# faith first

Legacy Edition
PARISH

## Grade Two

RESOURCES FOR CHRISTIAN LIVING®

www.FaithFirst.com

"The Ad Hoc Committee to Oversee the Use of the Catechism, United States Conference of Catholic Bishops, has found this catechetical series, copyright 2006, to be in conformity with the *Catechism of the Catholic Church*."

**NIHIL OBSTAT**
Reverend Robert M. Coerver
Censor Librorum

**IMPRIMATUR**
† Most Rev. Charles V. Grahmann
Bishop of Dallas

September 1, 2004

The Nihil Obstat and Imprimatur are official declarations that the material reviewed is free of doctrinal or moral error. No implication is contained therein that those granting the Nihil Obstat and Imprimatur agree with the contents, opinions, or statements expressed.

Send all inquiries to:
RCL • Resources for Christian Living
200 East Bethany Drive
Allen, Texas 75002-3804

Toll Free   877-275-4725
Fax            800-688-8356

Visit us at **www.RCLweb.com**
            **www.FaithFirst.com**

Printed in the United States of America

**20472**   ISBN 0-7829-1064-5 (Student Book)
**20482**   ISBN 0-7829-1076-9 (Catechist Guide)

1 2 3 4 5 6 7 8 9 10
05  06  07  08  09  10  11

**ACKNOWLEDGMENTS**

Scripture excerpts are taken or adapted from the *New American Bible with Revised New Testament and Psalms,* copyright © 1991, 1986, 1970, Confraternity of Christian Doctrine, Washington, DC. Used with permission. All rights reserved. No part of the *New American Bible* may be reproduced by any means without the permission of the copyright owner.

Excerpts are taken or adapted from the English translation of *Rite of Baptism for Children* © 1969, International Committee on English in the Liturgy, Inc. (ICEL); the English translation of *The Roman Missal* © 1973, ICEL; the English translation of *Rite of Confirmation, Second Edition* © 1975, ICEL; the English translation of the Act of Contrition from *Rite of Penance* © 1974, ICEL; excerpts from the English translation of *A Book of Prayers* © 1982, ICEL; excerpts from the English translation of *Book of Blessings* © 1988, ICEL. All rights reserved.

Excerpts are taken from the English translation of The Nicene Creed, Apostles' Creed, and *Gloria Patri* by the International Consultation on English Texts (ICET). All rights reserved.

Photograph and Illustration Credits appear on page 304.

# Faith First Legacy Edition Development Team

Developing a religion program requires the gifts and talents of many individuals working together as a team. RCL is proud to acknowledge the contributions of these dedicated people.

*Program Theology Consultants*
Reverend Louis J. Cameli, S.T.D.
Reverend Robert D. Duggan, S.T.D.

*Advisory Board*
Judith Deckers, M.Ed.
Elaine McCarron, SCN, M.Div.
Marina Herrera, Ph.D.
Reverend Frank McNulty, S.T.D.
Reverend Ronald J. Nuzzi, Ph.D.

*National Catechetical Advisor*
Jacquie Jambor

*Catechetical Specialist*
Jo Rotunno

*Contributing Writers*
*Student Book and Catechist Guide*
Christina DeCamp
Judith Deckers
Mary Beth Jambor
Marianne K. Lenihan
Michele Norfleet

*Art & Design Director*
Lisa Brent

*Electronic Page Makeup*
Laura Fremder

*Production Director*
Jenna Nelson

*Designers/Photo Research*
Pat Bracken
Kristy O. Howard
Susan Smith

*Project Editors*
Patricia A. Classick
Steven M. Ellair
Ronald C. Lamping

*Web Site Producers*
Joseph Crisalli
Demere Henson

*General Editor*
Ed DeStefano

*President/Publisher*
Maryann Nead

# Contents

## We Celebrate: The Liturgical Seasons

## We Pray

Dear God,
We think second grade will be lots of fun. There will be lots to do and learn. We will learn more about you, about Jesus, and about your Church. Help us to listen well, to take part in activities, and to do our best to love you and others each day.
Amen.

# Welcome to Faith First!

## A Quick Look at Me

*Make a nametag to tell others about yourself.*

- *In the middle, write in large letters what you like to be called.*
- *In each corner, write or draw these four things about yourself.*
  1. *A favorite story*
  2. *Something I like to do with my family*
  3. *My favorite holiday*
  4. *Something I do well*

# New Things to Learn

This year we will learn many new things about God. We will learn more about Jesus and about how to celebrate with our Church family.

Play this game with a partner to begin to learn new things. As you come to each lily pad, write the answer to the question.

## 1. We Believe

Jesus is God's own Son. He is the Savior of the world.

*Write the word that means "God saves."*

*Clue: Look on page 62.*

1.

Start

## 2. We Worship

At Mass we listen to God's word and give thanks to him.

*What is a word we sing before the Gospel at Mass?*

*Clue: Look on page 131.*

2.

## 4. We Pray

The Our Father is the prayer of the whole Church.

*What is another name for the Our Father?*

*Clue: Look on page 220.*

**4.**

Finish

## 3. We Live

God shares his life with us and helps us to live as his children.

*What is the name of the gift that makes us God's children?*

*Clue: Look on page 198.*

**3.**

# How Great Is Your Name!

LEADER: We gather to praise your name, O LORD.

ALL: O LORD, how great is your name.

LEADER: LORD, when I see the moon and all the stars you put in place, I wonder how you can remember us.

ALL: O LORD, how great is your name.

LEADER: But you made us little less than angels, You made us shepherds of all you made.

ALL: O LORD, how great is your name.

Based on Psalm 8:2, 4–7, 10

*Come forward and bow before the Bible.*

# Unit 1 • We Believe

*What does the Church ask us to believe?*

# Getting Ready

## What I Have Learned

What is something you already know about these three faith words?

God the Father

_____

_____

The Bible

_____

_____

The People of God

_____

_____

## Words to Know

Put an X next to the faith words you know. Put a ? next to the faith words you need to know more about.

**Faith Words**

_____ believe

_____ faith

_____ Holy Trinity

_____ Creator

_____ Gospels

_____ Pentecost

## A Question I Have

What question would you like to ask about the Holy Trinity?

_____

_____

## A Scripture Story

John the Baptist

What do you know about John the Baptist?

# We Know and Love God

## We Pray

Sing to God, all creation.

Based on Psalm 96:1

**O God, all your creation praises you. We ask you to bless us and to help us love you.        Amen.**

*How do you get to know more about your friends?*

Getting to know people is fun. God wants us to get to know him too. God tells us about himself in many ways.

*What are some ways you have come to know God?*

13

## Faith Focus

What are some ways God invites us to know and believe in him?

## Faith Words

**believe**
To believe in God means to know God and to give ourselves to him with all our heart.

**faith**
Faith is God's gift that makes us able to believe in him.

## Creation Tells Us About God

Creation is everything that God has made. All God's creation helps us to come to know and **believe** in God. All creation gives honor and glory to God.

People are the most important part of God's creation. All people are children of God. People are signs of God's love.

Our families and people in our Church help us to know and to love God. But it is God who tells us about himself. It is God who invites us to believe in him. It is God who invites us to give ourselves to him with all our heart.

 Finish the prayer. Thank God for the gifts of creation.

Thank you, God, for

_____

Thank you, God, for

_____

_____ .

## Jesus Tells Us About God

Jesus told us the most about God. One day a crowd of people came to Jesus. He told the people that they should believe in God with all their heart. He said,

> "Look at the birds. They have all the food they need. Your Father in heaven takes care of them. You are more important to God than the birds and all the animals."
>
> Based on Matthew 6:26

In this Bible story Jesus invites us to have **faith** in God. Faith is God's gift that makes us able to believe in him. When we say yes to God's invitation to believe in him, we have faith.

 What does the Bible story tell you about God? Tell a partner.

### Faith-Filled People

**Philip the Apostle**

Saint Philip was called by Jesus to be his follower. Jesus said to Philip, "Follow me." Philip became a follower of Jesus. Philip then went to his friend Nathanael and told him about Jesus. Nathanael believed too and became a follower of Jesus. The Church celebrates the feast day of Saint Philip on May 3.

## The Church Tells Us About God

Jesus gave us the Church to be a sign of God's love in the world. The Church is the community of the People of God who believe in Jesus Christ.

The Church helps us to grow in faith. We live our faith with our Church family. We live our faith every day.

We grow in faith with our Church community when we pray together. We grow in faith when we are kind to family, friends, and other people. We grow in faith when we care for God's creation. When we live our faith, we are signs of God's love for others.

*Draw a picture of someone who tells you about God.*

# Our Church Makes a Difference

## Our Parish Community

We belong to the Catholic Church. Our parish is our home in the Catholic Church.

Our parish family helps us to know and believe in God. Our parish family helps us to live our faith. Together we worship God. We listen to God's word. We give thanks to God for all his blessings. We care for God's creation. We are kind to people and treat them with respect. We share God's love with others.

 *Which of these things do you do with your parish community?*

### Our Catholic Faith

**The Parish Church**

Every Catholic parish has a name. The names of some parishes, such as Holy Trinity Parish, tell us about our faith in God. Others, such as Divine Savior Parish, tell us about our faith in Jesus. Other parishes are named after Mary and the other saints.

# What Difference Does Faith Make in My Life?

You are a sign of God's love. You can help other people to believe in God by what you say and what you do.

*Write your name on the invitation.
Fill in the answer card.*

## God Invites

_____
your name
_____

to know and believe in him.

## I Believe in God

## Dear God,

_____
_____.
_____
your name

## My Faith Choice

This week I will show I know and I love God. I will

_____
_____.

## We Believe in God!

*An act of faith tells God we believe in him.*
*Pray this act of faith as a class.*

**Leader:** Let us tell God we believe in him with all our heart.

**All:** **God, we believe in you with all our heart.**

**Group 1:** God our loving Father, all creation reminds us of your love.

**Group 2:** Jesus, Son of God, you showed us how much God loves us.

**Group 3:** God the Holy Spirit, you help us to know and love God.

**All:** **God, we believe in you with all our heart.**

## We Remember

*Complete the puzzle. Fill in the missing letters.*

Faith is

to k __ o __ God and

to b __ l __ e __ __ in

God with all our heart.

**To Help You Remember**

1. God gave us people and all creation to help us to know and believe in him.

2. God gave us Jesus to tell us the most about God.

3. God gave us the Church to help us come to know and believe in him.

## This Week . . .

In chapter 1, "We Know and Love God," your child learned that God reveals himself to us and invites us to believe in him. All creation helps us come to know and believe in God. Our families and people in our Church help us come to know and believe in God. Jesus told us the most about God. He invites us to have faith in God. Faith is God's gift that makes us able to believe in him. Jesus Christ is the greatest sign of God's love. We grow in faith and live our faith every day.

**For more** on the teachings of the Catholic Church on the mystery of divine Revelation and the gift of faith, see *Catechism of the Catholic Church* paragraph numbers 50–67, 84–95, and 142–175.

## Sharing God's Word

Read the Bible story in Matthew 6:26–34 about Jesus inviting the people to have faith in God or read the adaptation of the story on page 15. Emphasize that in this Bible story Jesus invites us to have faith in God.

## Praying

In this chapter your child learned to pray an act of faith. Read and pray together the prayer on page 19.

## Making a Difference

Choose one of the following activities to do as a family or design a similar activity of your own.

- All of creation is a sign of God's love. Take a walk outdoors. Look at all the wonderful things that God has created. Talk about what these things tell us about God.

- Name some of the people who help you come to know and believe in God. Write down their names. When you have finished, have each family member write a note of thanks to one person on the list.

- Learn more about the ways your parish helps you grow in faith. Thank God for your parish.

For more ideas on ways your family can live your faith, visit the "Faith First for Families" page at **www.FaithFirst.com**. You will find the "About Your Child" helpful as your child begins a new year.

# We Believe in the Holy Trinity

**2**

Stained-glass window showing the Church's belief in the Holy Trinity

## We Pray

Jesus prayed,
"Father, give them the Holy Spirit."
Based on Luke 11:13

**Glory to the Father, and to the Son, and to the Holy Spirit. Amen.**

*Do you like to solve mysteries?*

The Church teaches us about the mystery of God. We can never understand completely the mystery of God.

*What mystery about God does the Sign of the Cross tell us about?*

# One God in Three Persons

**Faith Focus**

What did Jesus tell us about who God is?

**Faith Words**

Holy Trinity
The Holy Trinity is one God in three Persons—God the Father, God the Son, and God the Holy Spirit.

soul
Our soul is that part of us that lives forever.

## God the Father

Jesus told us there is only one God who is God the Father, God the Son, and God the Holy Spirit. We call the one God in three Persons the **Holy Trinity.** The word *trinity* means "three in one."

God the Father is the first Person of the Holy Trinity. In the Apostles' Creed we pray,

"I believe in God the Father almighty, creator of heaven and earth."

God the Father created everyone and everything out of love. He created all people in his image and likeness. He created each person with a body and a **soul.** Our soul is that part of us that lives forever. God the Father loves us and cares for us. He creates us to be happy with him now and forever in heaven.

ACTIVITY *Jesus used the word Abba when he prayed to God the Father. Write the words Abba and Father on the lines. Use the words when you pray.*

_____

_____

## God the Son

God the Son is the second Person of the Holy Trinity. At Mass we pray, "We believe in one Lord, Jesus Christ, the only Son of God."

God the Father sent his Son to be one of us and live with us. Jesus is the Son of God. Jesus told us to call God our Father. He taught us that we are children of God. We are to live as children of God. Jesus said,

"Love God with all your heart. Love other people as much as you love yourself." Based on Matthew 22:37–39

 **ACTIVITY** *Learn to sign Jesus' message. Share it with others.*

**Love**     **God**     **with**

**all**     **your**     **heart.**

## God the Holy Spirit

God the Holy Spirit is the third Person of the Holy Trinity. At Mass we pray,

"We believe in the Holy Spirit, the Lord, the giver of life."

Jesus told us about the Holy Spirit. He told the disciples, "The Father in heaven will send you the Holy Spirit" (based on Luke 11:13). We first receive the gift of the Holy Spirit at Baptism. The priest or deacon says, "I baptize you in the name of the Father, and of the Son, and of the Holy Spirit." This shows that we share in the life of the Holy Trinity.

God sends us the Holy Spirit to help us to know and love God better. The Holy Spirit helps us to live as children of God.

*ACTIVITY Color the words in the rainbow banner. Thank God for telling you who he is.*

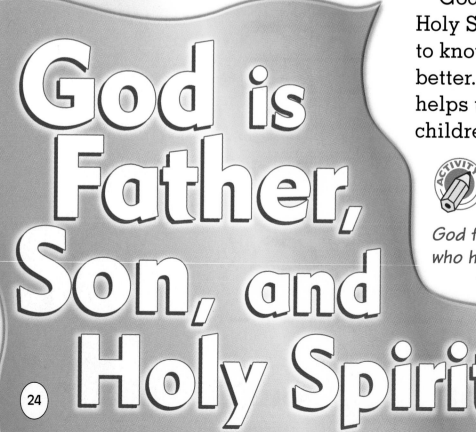

God is Father, Son, and Holy Spirit.

24

# Our Church Makes a Difference

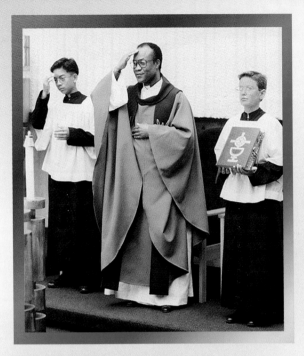

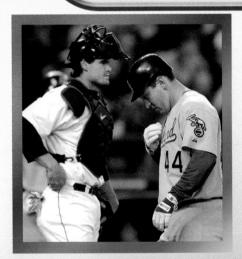

## Our Catholic Faith

### Sign of the Cross

We pray the Sign of the Cross at Mass. We begin Mass by blessing ourselves as we say the words. Before we listen to the Gospel we make a small Sign of the Cross on our forehead, on our lips, and over our heart. At the end of Mass, the priest makes the Sign of the Cross over the people and asks God to bless them.

## The Sign of the Cross

Catholics often pray the Sign of the Cross. We pray,
"In the name of the Father, and of the Son, and of the Holy Spirit. Amen."

As we say the words of the prayer, we bless ourselves. We touch our forehead, our shoulders, and our chest over our heart. We remember that we are baptized. We belong to God's family. We are to love God and all people as Jesus taught.

 *When do you pray the Sign of the Cross?*

# What Difference Does Faith Make in My Life?

God loves people so much. He wants everyone to know who he is.

*Saint Patrick used a shamrock to help people come to know the Holy Trinity. On each leaf of the shamrock, draw or write what you can tell others about the Holy Trinity.*

Father

Holy Spirit

Son

## My Faith Choice

I will tell others about the Holy Trinity this week. I will say

_____

_____.

## Signing Ourselves

*The Church uses many gestures, or actions, to help us to pray. Signing ourselves with a cross is one of the gestures the Church uses.*

**Leader:** Come forward one at a time. I will make a small sign of the cross on your forehead and say, "(Name), you belong to Christ." Then sign yourself and say, "I belong to Christ."

*(Name)*, you belong to Christ.

**Child:** **I belong to Christ.**

## We Remember

*Complete the sentences. Use the words in the word box.*

**one     three     Trinity**

1. We believe in the Holy

   _____ .

2. There is _____ God

   in _____ Persons.

### To Help You Remember

1. There is one God in three Persons. We call this the Holy Trinity.

2. God the Father is the first Person of the Holy Trinity.

3. God the Son is the second Person of the Holy Trinity.

4. God the Holy Spirit is the third Person of the Holy Trinity.

## This Week . . .

In chapter 2, "We Believe in the Holy Trinity," your child learned about the mystery of the Holy Trinity—the mystery of one God in three divine Persons: Father, Son, and Holy Spirit. We could never have come to know this wonderful truth about the identity of God on our own. Out of love, God revealed this about himself to us in Jesus Christ. The belief in the mystery of the Trinity is at the heart of the Church's living faith.

**For more** on the teachings of the Catholic Church on the mystery of the Trinity, see *Catechism of the Catholic Church* paragraph numbers 232–260.

## Sharing God's Word

Read together John 14:26 in which Jesus promised the disciples that the Holy Spirit would come to them. Emphasize that there is one God who is Father, Son, and Holy Spirit.

## Praying

In this chapter your child was signed with a cross. Use the prayer on page 27 and have family members sign one another with a cross in the morning or in the evening at bedtime.

## Making a Difference

Choose one of the following activities to do as a family or design a similar activity of your own.

- The Sign of the Cross helps us remember and express our faith in the Holy Trinity. Encourage your child to make the Sign of the Cross each time you pray.

- Create a Holy Trinity banner. Make three headings: Father, Son, and Holy Spirit. Under each heading write down what you know about each Person of the Holy Trinity or draw a symbol for each Person of the Trinity.

- Choose one way your family can reflect the love of the Holy Trinity to your neighbors or relatives.

For more ideas on ways your family can live your faith, visit the "Faith First for Families" page at **www.FaithFirst.com**. Click on "Games" and make learning fun for your child.

# God Is Our Father

## We Pray

Come, see
everything God
has done for us.
Based on Psalm 66:5

**God our Father,
bless us with
your gifts of
faith, hope, and
love.          Amen.**

*How do family
members show their
trust in one another?*

The Bible and our
Church teach us that
God is our Father.
We believe in him
and trust him.

*What have you
learned about God
our Father?*

# God Our Creator and Father

## Faith Focus

Why do we call God our Father?

## Faith Words

**Creator**
God alone is the Creator. God has made everyone and everything out of love and without any help.

**almighty**
God alone is almighty. This means that only God has the power to do everything.

## God the Creator

You are getting to know more and more about God. God the Father is the **Creator.** He made everyone and everything out of love and without any help. He made the creatures we can see and the angels we cannot see.

God tells us the story of creation. It is the first story in the Bible.

In the beginning God created the heavens and the earth. He made the sun, the other stars, and the moon. He made the sky, the earth, and the sea.

God made plants, trees, and flowers. He made all the fish and the birds. He made all the animals and other creatures that live on the land. Then God created people in his image and likeness.

God looked at all that he had created. He saw that it was very good.
Based on Genesis 1:1, 7–12, 16, 20–21, 24–25, 27, 31

**QUESTION?** *What does creation tell you about God the Creator?*

## God the Almighty

We can learn about God when we look at creation. We see how much God loves us.

As we get to know God more, we learn that God is **almighty.** This means that only God has the power to do everything.

God tells us that he does everything out of love. God is always good and loving. We believe in and love God the Father with all our heart. We show God and others our trust and love for him.

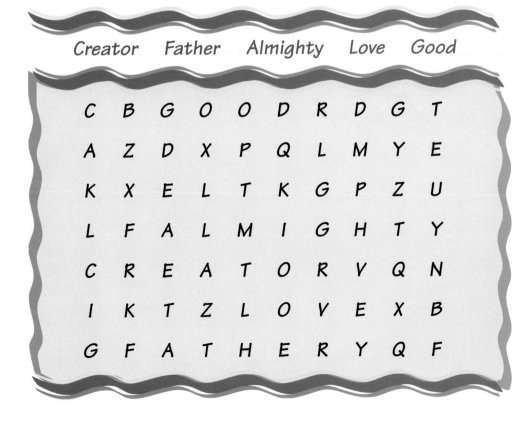

## Faith-Filled People

### Bonaventure

Saint Bonaventure looked at creation and came to know and love God. He said that creation was like a mirror. Whenever he looked at creation, he saw a good and loving God. The Church celebrates the feast day of Saint Bonaventure on July 15.

*Find and circle the words that tell about God. What does each word tell you about God?*

*Creator    Father    Almighty    Love    Good*

| | | | | | | | | |
|---|---|---|---|---|---|---|---|---|
| C | B | G | O | O | D | R | D | G | T |
| A | Z | D | X | P | Q | L | M | Y | E |
| K | X | E | L | T | K | G | P | Z | U |
| L | F | A | L | M | I | G | H | T | Y |
| C | R | E | A | T | O | R | V | Q | N |
| I | K | T | Z | L | O | V | E | X | B |
| G | F | A | T | H | E | R | Y | Q | F |

## God Our Father

Jesus told us the most about God. One day Jesus' friends asked him to teach them to pray. He taught them to pray,

"Our Father in heaven
    hallowed be your name."

Matthew 6:9

Jesus taught that God the Father is our Father. He loves and cares for us. He knows what we need before we ask for it. God always does what is best for us. We are to believe in him and trust him.

 *When you pray the Our Father, what picture comes to your mind? Draw it here.*

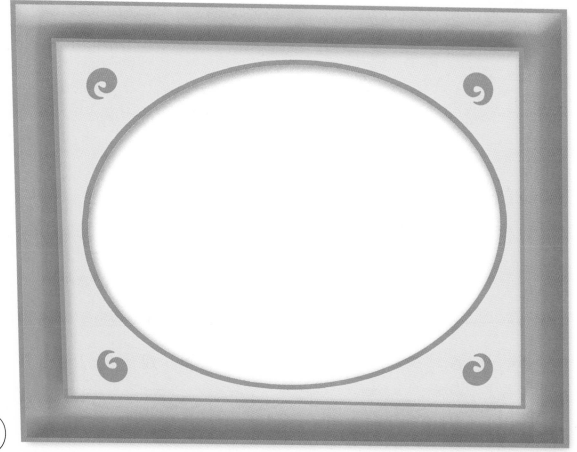

## Saint Augustine's Garden

The children of Saint Augustine's School honor God the Father and Creator in a special way. They grow vegetables and food in a garden at Saint Augustine's School.

They plant the seeds. They harvest their crops. They wash and bag the fruits and vegetables, and take the food to a food bank.

As they work in the garden, the children feel close to God. They show their love for God and people when they take care of creation.

**QUESTION** *How do you and your friends care for creation?*

### Our Catholic Faith

**The Lord's Prayer**

The Our Father is the prayer of all Christians. It is called the Our Father because these are the first words of the prayer. The Our Father is also called the Lord's Prayer because Jesus our Lord gave this prayer to the Church.

# What Difference Does Faith Make in My Life?

God created everyone and everything out of love. God shares the gift of his love with you every day.

*Draw yourself with the gifts of God's creation. Be sure to include other people.*

## Gifts of God's Creation

**My Faith Choice**

This week I will show my love for others. I will

_____

_____ .

# Praising God
# A Scripture Story

## We Pray

Sing to God for all
the good things
of the earth.
Based on Psalm 33:3, 5

**Blessed are you,
God the Creator.
Everything good
comes from you!
Amen.**

*What are some
ways you show
others how you feel?*

Sometimes we use
more than words to
tell others how we
think and feel.
Sometimes we use
music and singing
to praise and give
thanks to God.

*When do you use
music and singing
to praise God?*

# Bible Background

Why do we pray the Psalms?

**psalms**
Psalms are songs of prayer.

**prayer of praise**
A prayer of praise gives honor to God for his great love and kindness.

## We Sing to God

People pray in many ways. People pray alone and with others. People pray aloud and they pray silently. Sometimes people sing their prayers.

The Bible has many prayers that God's people sang. These prayers are called **psalms.** They are found in the Book of Psalms in the Old Testament. There are 150 psalms in the Book of Psalms.

God's people prayed many kinds of psalms. Some of the Psalms they prayed are **prayers of praise**. They honor God for his great love and his kindness.

*Draw a picture about creation that helps you to praise God.*

Give Praise to God

38

# Reading the Word of God

## We Praise God

Psalm 148 is a psalm of praise. The beautiful words of this psalm almost make music. Listen for the sound of the words as we pray,

Praise God, all you angels.
Praise him, sun and moon;
   give praise, all shining stars.
Praise the LORD, you mountains
   and hills.
Praise God, all animals
  that live on the land and that live
  in the water.
All people, young and old, lift up
  your hearts.
All praise the name of God.
          Based on Psalm 148:2–3, 9–13

*Look at the picture you drew on page 38. Close your eyes. See your favorite part of creation. Hear the sounds of creation. Quietly praise God in your heart.*

## The Psalms

The writers of the Psalms wrote many kinds of psalms. They wrote some psalms for people to pray when they are happy. They wrote other psalms for people to pray when they are sad.

There are also psalms for people to pray when they want to ask God's help or forgiveness. There are other psalms to help people tell God they love him. Some psalms, such as Psalm 148, help people to praise God for everything he does for them.

**ACTIVITY** *Clap your hands as you pray aloud the lyrics of this song.*

### God Is Always with Us

God    is    with    us    day    to    day.

God    is    with    us    when    we    play.

God    is    with    us    when    we    pray.

God,    I    love    you    in    every    way.

## Christians Sing to God

Saint Francis of Assisi loved to sing about God. He sang a song that Christians still sing today. It is called "The Canticle of the Sun." Here is part of the song Saint Francis sang.

Be praised, my Lord,
  with all your creatures,
  especially Brother Sun!
Be praised, my Lord,
  for Sister Moon and Stars!
  They are bright and lovely and fair.
Be praised, my Lord,
  for Brother Wind, and for Air and
  Weather, cloudy and clear.

Today we can listen to Christian songs on CDs and on the radio. Christian singers sing of God's love and goodness. Many of their songs remind us to live as Jesus taught us.

 *Pretend you are a Christian singer. What would you sing about? Share your ideas with a partner.*

### Our Catholic Faith

**Responsorial Psalm**

Every day the Church prays the Psalms. After the first reading at Mass, the cantor, or song leader, leads us in singing or praying a psalm aloud.

# What Difference Does Faith Make in My Life?

God's love filled the hearts of the writers of the Psalms and Saint Francis of Assisi. God's love fills your heart too.

*Each Sunday at Mass you join with your parish in singing to God. Create a cover for a CD for one of your favorite hymns.*

## My Faith Choice

This week I will lift up my heart in song to God. I will sing about

_____

_____.

## Praying a Psalm

*The Church prays the Psalms every day.
Join with the Church and pray this verse
of Psalm 147.*

**Leader:** Let us give praise to God.
**All:** **How good to celebrate our God in song.**

**Leader:** God is kind and good.
**All:** **How good to celebrate our God in song.**

Psalm 147:1

## We Remember

*Read each sentence. Color the ◯ next to each correct sentence.*

◯ Psalms tell God how good he is.

◯ Psalms help us to tell God we love and trust him.

◯ Catholics pray the Psalms at Mass.

**To Help You Remember**

1. Psalms are prayers we sing.

2. Some of the Psalms give praise and thanks to God.

3. Some of the Psalms help us to pray for other people and for ourselves.

# With My Family

**4**

## This Week . . .

In chapter 4, "Praising God: A Scripture Story," your child learned about the Psalms. Praying the Psalms is a key form of Christian prayer. The Psalms have been prayed since Jesus' time as the public prayer of the Church. There are 150 psalms in the Book of Psalms, which is found in the Old Testament. Psalms express our prayer in many forms. Some of the Psalms bless and give adoration to God. Others give thanks to God for his love and kindness. Others are prayers asking God for help and forgiveness. Others praise God for the good things he has done for us and has given us.

**For more** on the teachings of the Catholic Church on the Psalms, singing and music, and Christian prayer, see *Catechism of the Catholic Church* paragraph numbers 1156–1158, 2623–2643, and 2700–2704.

## Sharing God's Word

Read together Psalm 148 or the adaptation of the verses from Psalm 148 on page 39. Emphasize that the Psalms are prayers and that Psalm 148 is a prayer to God, praising him for all creation.

## Praying

In this chapter your child prayed a prayer using Psalm 147:1. Read and pray together the prayer on page 43.

## Making a Difference

Choose one of the following activities to do as a family or design a similar activity of your own.

- Ask each family member to share a favorite song that praises God. Choose one that you can all sing together. Sing it at dinnertime this week.

- Make a book illustrating Psalm 148. Adaptations of verses from Psalm 148 are on page 39.

- There are some excellent contemporary Christian music groups that perform powerful praise music. Search the Internet or a local music store to find something your child likes. Listen to this music with your child.

For more ideas on ways your family can live your faith, visit the "Faith First for Families" page at **www.FaithFirst.com**. Click on "Family Prayer" for a prayer you can pray as a family this week.

# Jesus Is the Son of God

**5**

## We Pray

Rejoice, the Prince
of Peace is born.
Based on Isaiah 9:5

**God our Father,
thank you
for sending us
Jesus, your Son.
Amen.**

*How does your
family celebrate
Christmas?*

Each year at
Christmas we
remember that God
fulfilled a special
promise.

*What promise do
we celebrate at
Christmas?*

Statues from a
Christmas crèche

45

# God's Special Promise

## Faith Focus

How does Jesus show us God's love and mercy?

## Faith Words

**Covenant**
The Covenant is God's promise always to love and be kind to his people.

**Jesus Christ**
Jesus Christ is the Son of God. He is the second Person of the Holy Trinity who became one of us. He is true God and true man.

## God Keeps His Promise

The Bible tells us about a promise God made to his people. We call this promise the **Covenant.** This promise shows that God always loves and is kind to people.

God's Covenant with people began at creation. Our first parents broke the promises they made to God. They sinned. We call this sin original sin.

God made the Covenant again with Noah and with Abraham and with Moses. God's people still sometimes broke the Covenant. When God's people broke their part of the Covenant, God promised to send someone to make God and people friends again.

God kept his promise. He sent **Jesus Christ.** Jesus Christ is the Son of God. He is the new and everlasting Covenant. He is the second Person of the Holy Trinity who became one of us. Jesus is true God and true man.

**QUESTION** *What does the Covenant tell about God and God's love?*

## Jesus Is Born

The Bible tells us about the birth of Jesus. We call this story the Nativity. Act out this play about the Nativity.

**Narrator**    Just before Jesus' birth, Joseph and Mary traveled to Bethlehem. Mary and Joseph stopped to find a room at an inn.

**Action**    *Joseph knocks on the door of the inn. The innkeeper opens the door.*

**Joseph**    Do you have a room for my wife and me?

**Innkeeper**    There are no rooms left. You may stay in the stable.

**Narrator**    Mary and Joseph went to the stable. Jesus was born there.
Based on Luke 2:5–7

## Glory to God!

**Shepherds' Words**

_____

_____

**My Words**

_____

_____

ACTIVITY The Bible tells us that angels told shepherds about the birth of Jesus. Write the words of joy the shepherds might have said. Write your own words of joy.

## God Cares for All People

The Bible tells us that when Jesus grew up, he traveled from place to place. He taught about God's mercy and love. The word *mercy* means "great kindness." Read this Bible story about God's mercy.

People followed Jesus from the towns. As nighttime came, Jesus saw that the people were hungry. The disciples had only two fish and five loaves of bread to feed all the people. Jesus took the food, looked to heaven, and blessed the food. Then he gave the food to his disciples to give to the people. Everyone had enough to eat. There was even food left over.

Based on Matthew 14:13, 15–17, 19–20

*How do you show kindness to others? Share how you are a sign of God's love when you are kind to people.*

# Our Church Makes a Difference

## Build a World of Kindness

The Church teaches people about God's mercy when the Church cares for people. The Church cares for people in many ways.

We help people build and repair homes. We take care of people who are sick. We share our clothes with people who cannot buy clothes. We give food and water to people who are hungry and thirsty.

When we do these and other kind things, we treat others as Jesus did. We treat others as God does. We do works of mercy. We help build a world of kindness and love.

_____

**ACTIVITY**
*Write how the people in these pictures are sharing God's love.*

_____

_____

# What Difference Does Faith Make in My Life?

Jesus is the greatest sign of God's love and mercy. You are a follower of Jesus. The Holy Spirit helps you to live as a sign of God's love and mercy.

*You hear stories about people caring for others. Write a story about one of these pictures. Share your story with a partner.*

Story title _____

Where did it happen? _____

When did it happen? _____

Who was there? _____

_____

What happened? _____

_____

## My Faith Choice

This week I will live as a sign of God's love and mercy. I will

_____

_____ .

## The Angelus

*The Angelus is a prayer that praises God for the birth of Jesus. Pray this part of the prayer together.*

**Group 1:** The angel spoke God's message to Mary,

**Group 2:** and she conceived of the Holy Spirit.

**All:** **Hail Mary . . .**

**Group 1:** "I am the lowly servant of the Lord:

**Group 2:** let it be done to me according to your word."

**All:** **Hail Mary . . .**

**Group 1:** And the Word became flesh

**Group 2:** and lived among us.

**All:** **Hail Mary . . .**

## We Remember

*Add letters to complete the words in the sentences.*

1. M ___ ___ ___ is the mother of Jesus.

2. ___ ___ s ___ ___ is the Son of God.

3. Jesus showed us God's love and

   ___ ___ r ___ y.

### To Help You Remember

1. The Covenant is a sign of God's love and mercy.

2. The birth of Jesus Christ, the Son of God, is a sign of God's love and mercy.

3. Everything Jesus said and did shows us God's love and mercy.

 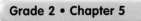

## This Week . . .

In chapter 5, "Jesus Is the Son of God," your child learned about the Covenant that God entered into with his people. The Covenant is a sign of God's love and mercy. The Covenant was first made with people at creation. When Adam and Eve sinned and broke the Covenant, God promised to send someone to renew the Covenant. God fulfilled his promise by sending the Son of God, Jesus Christ, who became man and lived among us. Jesus Christ is true God and true man. He is the new and everlasting Covenant.

**For more** on the teachings of the Catholic Church on the Covenant and the mystery of the Incarnation, see *Catechism of the Catholic Church* paragraph numbers 51–67 and 456–560.

## Sharing God's Word

Read together the Bible story in Luke 2:1–14 about Jesus' birth or read the play about the Nativity on page 47. Emphasize that Jesus Christ is the Son of God.

## Praying

In this chapter your child prayed part of the Angelus. Read and pray together the prayer on page 51.

## Making a Difference

Choose one of the following activities to do as a family or design a similar activity of your own.

- Read together the Bible story on page 48, which is about Jesus feeding the people. Talk about how the hungry people must have felt when they realized that Jesus gave everyone more than enough to eat.

- Everything Jesus did was a sign of God's love. Choose to do one thing together this week to live as signs of God's love.

- [Jesus told] people over and over again a[bout G]od's love for them. Look around you[r ho]me for something that reminds you [of] God's love.

For more ideas on ways your family can live your faith, visit the "Faith First for Families" page at **www.FaithFirst.com**. You will find the "Contemporary Issues" page helpful this week.

# John the Baptist
## A Scripture Story

## We Pray

Blessed be God,
who has come to
save his people.
Based on Psalm 111:2, 9

**Lord our God,
speak to us.
Help us to know
you.          Amen.**

*What does your
family do to get
ready when visitors
are coming?*

The Bible has many
stories of people
who helped others
get ready for Jesus.

*Why were the
people of the Bible
waiting for Jesus?*

# Bible Background

## Faith Focus

What did John the Baptist tell the people?

## Faith Words

prophet
A prophet in the Bible is a person who God chose to speak in his name.

## The Work of John the Baptist

There are stories in the Bible about people who helped others get ready for Jesus. John the Baptist was one of those people. John was the son of Elizabeth and Zechariah.

**ACTIVITY** Pretend you are one of the people in the group. You are looking for John the Baptist. Follow the maze and lead the people to John. What question would you ask John when you reach him?

## John Gets the People Ready

Many people believed John was a **prophet.** A prophet is a person God chooses to speak in his name. God chose John the Baptist to tell the people that Jesus was the Savior he had promised to send. Many people came to John the Baptist to listen to his message. John told the people,

"Someone will soon be coming. You must get ready for him. Sin no more." Some of the people told John, "We are sorry for our sins." John told them, "You need to ask God for forgiveness." John invited them into the river and he baptized them.

One day Jesus came to John. John baptized Jesus. He told the people, "This is the One God promised to send. He is the Son of God."
Based on Matthew 3:2–3, 5–6 and John 1:29, 34

**QUESTION** *What is one thing you can do to help someone come to know Jesus better?*

# Understanding the Word of God

## We Prepare for Jesus

The people listened to John and began to prepare to welcome Jesus. We also need to prepare ourselves to welcome Jesus into our lives.

We prepare for Jesus by listening to God's word and by praying. When we do, we come to know Jesus better. We learn to love God above all else. We try to live as God's children.

 *Write what you could do this week to prepare to welcome Jesus into your life.*

# Our Church Makes a Difference

## We Hear God's Word at Mass

When we listen to the Bible readings at Mass, we are listening to God. At Mass on Sunday a member of the parish community proclaims the first two readings. We call the people who do this readers, or lectors. The deacon or priest proclaims the Gospel.

After the Gospel is proclaimed, the priest or deacon preaches a homily. This helps us to understand God's word to us. We learn more and more about God and his mercy and love. We learn to share God's love and mercy with people.

**QUESTION ?** *What is one thing you have learned about Jesus at Mass?*

### Our Catholic Faith

**Ambo**

The Church proclaims God's word at every Mass. The ambo is the place in the church where God's word is proclaimed. This place is also called the lectern. The ambo, or lectern, is often made of the same material as the altar.

57

# What Difference Does Faith Make in My Life?

You can help others come to know more and more about Jesus as John the Baptist did. The Holy Spirit helps you to tell others about Jesus.

*Write one thing about Jesus that you would like to tell a friend or someone in your family. Tell why you want to share that message with them.*

## Telling People About Jesus

Just as John the Baptist did, I would like to tell people that Jesus

_____

_____ .

I will share this because

_____

_____ .

## My Faith Choice

This week I will tell others about Jesus. I will say

_____

_____ .

# Jesus Is Our Savior

## We Pray

LORD, out of love, you promised to save us.
Based on Psalm 119:41

**Jesus, you are the Savior of the world.** **Amen.**

*Who in your community helps people who are in danger?*

A firefighter might save someone from a burning house. God sent his only Son to save us from our sins.

*What did Jesus do to save us from our sins?*

# God Fulfills His Promise

Why do we call Jesus Christ the Savior of all people?

## Faith Words

**Crucifixion**
The Crucifixion is the death of Jesus on a cross.

**Resurrection**
The Resurrection is God's raising Jesus from the dead to new life.

## God Sends the Savior

God promised to send his people a savior. A savior is a person who sets people free. God the Father sent his Son, Jesus, to be the Savior of the world. Read this Bible story. It is the announcement that the time had come when God would fulfill his promise to send the Savior.

An angel came to Joseph before Jesus was born. The angel said to Joseph, "Mary, your wife, will give birth to a son. You are to give him the name Jesus. He will save his people from their sins. All this will happen to fulfill God's promises."

Based on Matthew 1:20–23

The name *Jesus* means "God saves." Jesus died on the cross to free us from our sins. God's forgiveness is a sign of his mercy and love.

 *Color the name Jesus. Say a prayer thanking Jesus for his love.*

# JESUS

## Jesus Dies on the Cross

Acts and words of forgiveness are signs of love. Jesus showed his love for his Father and for us by freely dying on the cross. We call Jesus' death on the cross the **Crucifixion.** Read this part of what happened at the Crucifixion.

> The soldiers put Jesus to death on a cross on a hill near the city of Jerusalem. The name of the hill is Calvary. The sky became very dark. Jesus said, "Father, forgive them." Then Jesus died.
>
> Based on Luke 23:33–34, 44, 46

Jesus' death on the cross freed us from sin and death. Jesus has made us friends with God again. We can live forever with God in heaven. Jesus is the Savior of the world.

 *Why is the cross a sign of Jesus' love for all people?*

## Jesus Is Raised to New Life

Three days after Jesus died, Mary Magdalene and two other women disciples of Jesus went to the place where Jesus was buried. When they arrived there, the women saw that the body of Jesus was not there. God raised Jesus to new life. We call this the **Resurrection** of Jesus. Read what happened.

Two men dressed in bright white robes appeared to them and said, "Jesus is not here. He has been raised." They left the tomb and told the Apostles and others what happened. Peter and the others did not believe them. So they rushed to the tomb to see for themselves if what the women disciples said was true.

Based on Luke 24:4, 6, 9, 11–12

We too shall live after we die. We will live in happiness with God, and with Mary and all the saints forever in heaven.

*ACTIVITY*

*Connect the dots. Discover a word that means "Praise God." Learn the word and pray it in the morning and at bedtime.*

## The Easter Candle

The Crucifixion and the Resurrection are the greatest signs of God's love and mercy. We light the Easter candle to remind us that the Risen Jesus is the Savior of the world.

We see the Easter candle near the altar at Mass. We see it near the baptismal font or pool during the celebration of Baptism.

We use other lighted candles in our parish church too. Lighted candles remind us that Jesus was raised from the dead and he is always with us.

**?** *Where do you see lighted candles in your parish church? Find out why the candles are in those places.*

### Our Catholic Faith

**The Crucifix**

The crucifix is also a sign of God's love and mercy. The crucifix is a cross with an image of Jesus on it. In our churches the crucifix is near the altar. Many families have a crucifix in their homes. Some Christians wear a crucifix on a chain around their neck.

Blessing of water at the Easter Vigil

# What Difference Does Faith Make in My Life?

Jesus is the Savior of all people. He is always with us. The Holy Spirit invites you to share this good news with everyone.

*Design this bookmark with colors and pictures that help you remember Jesus is the Savior of the world.*

**Christ has died!**

**Christ is risen!**

**Christ will come again!**

**Alleluia!**

## My Faith Choice

 This week I will share the story of God's love with others. I will

_____

_____ .

## We Pray

### Acclamation

*Acclamations are prayers of praise. We pray acclamations to praise God for all the wonderful things he has done. Pray this acclamation that we pray aloud or sing at Mass.*

**Leader:** Let us proclaim the mystery of faith.

**All:** **Christ has died,
Christ is risen,
Christ will come again. Alleluia.**

## We Remember

*Use the words in the box to complete the sentences.*

> **Savior   Resurrection   Crucifixion**

1. God raising Jesus to new life is

   called the _____.

2. God sent Jesus to be the

   _____.

3. Jesus' death on a cross is called the

   _____.

### To Help You Remember

1. Jesus Christ is the Savior God promised to send us.

2. Jesus was crucified and freely died on the cross to save all people from their sins.

3. Jesus was raised from the dead by God to new life.

## This Week . . .

In chapter 7, "Jesus Is Our Savior," your child learned that Jesus is the Savior of all people. Our salvation flows from God's initiative of love and mercy. Because God loves us, he sent the Son of God who freely died to free all people from sin. We call this saving event the Crucifixion. God raised Jesus from the dead to a new and glorified life. We call this event the Resurrection. We too shall live after we die. God invites us to live an eternal life of happiness with him and with Mary and all the saints.

**For more** on the teachings of the Catholic Church on the mystery of Jesus Christ and God's loving plan of salvation, see *Catechism of the Catholic Church* paragraph numbers 422–451, 456–478, and 599–655.

## Sharing God's Word

Read the Bible story about the angel who came to Joseph before Jesus was born. You can find this story on page 62 or in Matthew 1:20–23. Emphasize that the angel came to announce that the time had come for God to fulfill his promises.

## Praying

In this chapter your child learned to pray a memorial acclamation. Read and pray together the prayer on page 67.

## Making a Difference

Choose one of the following activities to do as a family or design a similar activity of your own.

- The crucifix reminds us of God's love for us. Talk about how your family reminds each other about God's love.

- When you go to Mass this week, pay close attention to the Memorial Acclamation. Use the acclamation you sang at Mass for family prayer at home.

- The lighted Easter candle is the most important candle our Church uses. We use other candles too. All lighted candles remind us that the Risen Jesus is always with us. This week when you go to Mass, notice where you see lighted candles used in your parish.

For more ideas on ways your family can live your faith, visit the "Faith First for Families" page at **www.FaithFirst.com**. You will find the "Contemporary Issues" page helpful this week.

# The Traveler on the Road to Emmaus

## A Scripture Story

## We Pray

"I am with you always."
Matthew 28:20

Holy Spirit, help us to share the good news of Jesus' Resurrection.
Amen.

When have you missed someone who went away?

After Jesus died, the disciples missed him very much. Three days later, they saw him again!

Why did the disciples get to see Jesus again?

The Risen Jesus with two disciples on the road to Emmaus

69

# Bible Background

## Faith Focus

What does the Gospel story about walking to the village of Emmaus teach us?

## Faith Words

**Apostles**
The Apostles were the disciples who Jesus chose and sent to preach the Gospel to the whole world in his name.

**Gospels**
The Gospels are the first four books in the New Testament.

## The Four Gospels

The Church shares the faith stories that the **Apostles** and the first Christians told about Jesus. These stories are found in the four **Gospels.** The word *gospel* means "good news." The Gospels share the good news about Jesus with the world.

The Gospels are the first four books in the New Testament. The New Testament is the second main part of the Bible. The most important stories in the New Testament are the Gospel stories of the suffering, death, and Resurrection of Jesus Christ.

 *In these boxes draw a Bible story you know about Jesus. Share it with a partner and your family.*

## The Traveler to Emmaus

Two of Jesus' disciples were walking to the village of Emmaus. It was three days after Jesus died and was buried. The Gospel of Luke tells what happened.

The Risen Jesus began to walk along with them. They did not recognize Jesus. When they came close to Emmaus, they invited Jesus to stay with them. They sat down for a meal and Jesus took the bread. He thanked and blessed God, broke the bread, and shared it with them. Suddenly, the disciples recognized that the traveler who had been with them was the Risen Jesus.

Based on Luke 24:15–16, 28–31

This Gospel story shares that the Risen Jesus is alive in a new way. He is always with us.

**When does the Church break and share bread?**

# Understanding the Word of God

Bread was very important to the early Christians. Look at these pictures to see how bread was made.

1. Cutting the wheat

2. Grinding the wheat

## The Breaking of Bread

The two disciples recognized the Risen Jesus when he broke bread and shared it with them. This was what Jesus also did at the Last Supper. The Last Supper is the last meal Jesus ate with his disciples before he died.

The early Christians used the words "the breaking of bread" for the Eucharist. Jesus is with us in a most special way when we celebrate the Eucharist. The bread and wine become the Body and Blood of Christ. We receive Jesus in Holy Communion.

Bible stories about breaking and sharing bread remind us that God is always with his people. God always takes care of his people.

**QUESTION?** *When does the priest break the consecrated bread at Mass?*
*Clue: Turn to page 294.*

3. Kneading the bread dough

4. Baking the bread

# Our Church Makes a Difference

## The Bread of Life

At Mass the priest breaks and shares the consecrated bread, the Body of Christ. As the priest breaks the bread, he prays aloud, "Lamb of God, you take away the sins of the world." Jesus Christ is the Lamb of God. He is the Savior of the world.

The breaking of the consecrated bread at Mass shows that we all share one Bread, Jesus, the Bread of Life. Receiving Jesus, the Bread of Life, in Holy Communion joins us more closely to him and to one another. We receive the grace to live as followers of Jesus. We live as Jesus taught and help people in need.

 *What is one way your parish helps people in need?*

73

# What Difference Does Faith Make in My Life?

At Mass we receive the Body and Blood of Christ. Jesus, the Bread of Life, shares himself with us. The Holy Spirit invites you to share your talents with others.

*Who are some of the people who help you to know that Jesus is with you? Write their names and tell what they do.*

## "I Am Always With You"

| Name | What They Do |
|------|--------------|
| _____ | _____ |
|  | _____ |
| _____ | _____ |
|  | _____ |

## My Faith Choice

This week I will be a sign that Jesus is always with us. I will

_____

_____.

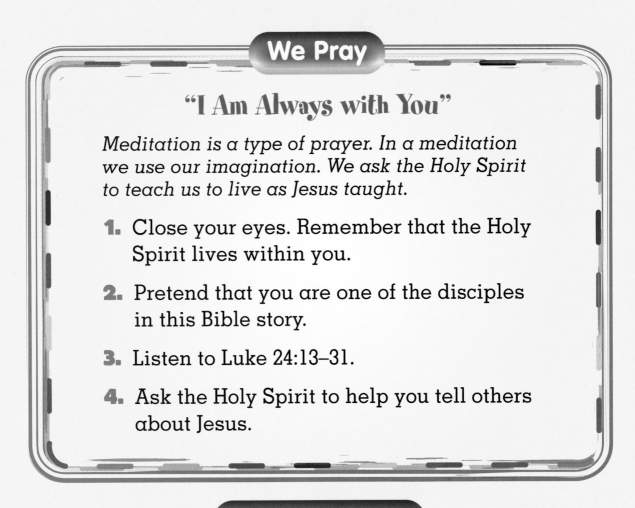

## We Pray

### "I Am Always with You"

*Meditation is a type of prayer. In a meditation we use our imagination. We ask the Holy Spirit to teach us to live as Jesus taught.*

1. Close your eyes. Remember that the Holy Spirit lives within you.

2. Pretend that you are one of the disciples in this Bible story.

3. Listen to Luke 24:13–31.

4. Ask the Holy Spirit to help you tell others about Jesus.

## We Remember

*Number the sentences in the order the events take place in the Gospel story.*

_____ The disciples invited Jesus to share a meal with them.

_____ Jesus blessed, broke, and shared the bread with them.

_____ Jesus met two disciples on their way to Emmaus.

_____ The disciples recognized the Risen Jesus.

### To Help You Remember

1. The four Gospels share with us the teachings and life of Jesus.

2. The most important stories in the Gospels are about the death and Resurrection of Jesus.

3. At Mass the bread and wine become the Body and Blood of Jesus. He is really with us.

## This Week . . .

In chapter 8, "The Traveler on the Road to Emmaus: A Scripture Story," your child learned that our Church shares the faith stories that the Apostles and the first Christians told about Jesus. These stories are found in the four Gospels. The Gospel story of two disciples walking to Emmaus shares that Jesus was raised from the dead and is alive in a new way. Jesus is with us in a unique way at Mass. At Mass the bread and wine become the Body and Blood of Christ. We receive Jesus, the Bread of Life, in Holy Communion.

**For more** on the teachings of the Catholic Church on the mystery of Christ's presence with the Church, see *Catechism of the Catholic Church* paragraph numbers 610–611 and 1356–1405.

## Sharing God's Word

Read together the Bible story in Luke 24:13–31 about the disciples who were walking to the village of Emmaus or read the adaptation of the story on page 71. Emphasize that at Mass the bread and wine become the Body and Blood of Christ and Jesus is really with us.

## Praying

In this chapter your child prayed a meditation prayer. Pray together the meditation on page 75.

## Making a Difference

Choose one of the following activities to do as a family or design a similar activity of your own.

• Look on the Internet or at your public library for pictures of the Holy Land. Look for the village of Emmaus and the city of Jerusalem. Talk about what it might have been like to walk from Jerusalem to Emmaus.

• The Bible story in this chapter reminds us how important it is for us to share meals together. Talk about ways your family can make everyday meals together special.

• Make a loaf of homemade bread and eat it together. Talk about how the disciples recognized the Risen Jesus when he broke the bread and shared it with them. Relate this story to the celebration of the Eucharist.

For more ideas on ways your family can live your faith, visit the "Faith First for Families" page at **www.FaithFirst.com**. This week you will find it useful to visit "Questions Kids Ask" and discuss the question.

# The Holy Spirit

## We Pray

LORD God, send us
   your Spirit,
   and renew all the
   earth.
   Based on Psalm 104:30

**Come, Holy
Spirit, fill our
hearts with your
love. Amen.**

*What are some
times when you
have needed help
from others?*

Every Christian
needs help to live
as a follower of
Jesus. Jesus sent
the Holy Spirit to
help us.

*What do you
know about the
Holy Spirit?*

# God's Gift of Love

## Faith Focus

What does the New Testament tell us about the Holy Spirit?

## Faith Words

**Ascension**
The Ascension is the return of the Risen Jesus to his Father in heaven forty days after the Resurrection.

**Pentecost**
Pentecost is the day the Holy Spirit came to the disciples of Jesus, fifty days after the Resurrection.

## The Promise of the Holy Spirit

Jesus promised that the Father would send the Holy Spirit to be our helper. The Holy Spirit is the third Person of the Holy Trinity.

Jesus made this promise before he returned to his Father in heaven. We call the return of the Risen Jesus to his Father in heaven the **Ascension**. This happened forty days after the Resurrection. Jesus said,

"I am sending the promise of my Father to you. It is the gift of the Holy Spirit." Based on Luke 24:49

The Holy Spirit is always with us.

 *Decorate this postcard. Share Jesus' promise with your family and friends.*

## Sharing the Promise

## Pentecost

Jesus' promise came true fifty days after the Resurrection. The day that the Holy Spirit came to the Apostles is called **Pentecost.** This is what the Bible tells us happened.

After Jesus returned to his Father, the disciples and Mary, the mother of Jesus, were praying together in a room. Suddenly, a big sound filled the house. It was the sound of a strong wind. Small flames settled over each disciple's head. The disciples were all filled with the Holy Spirit. Peter and the disciples then left the house. They went to tell others about Jesus.

Based on Acts of the Apostles 2:1–4, 14, 22

We first receive the gift of the Holy Spirit at Baptism. The Holy Spirit helps us tell others about Jesus as Peter did.

 *What is one thing you want to tell someone about Jesus?*

## The Holy Spirit Is Always with Us

The Holy Spirit helps us to believe and trust in God the Father and in Jesus Christ. The Holy Spirit helps us to live as children of God and followers of Jesus.

The Holy Spirit helps us to pray. When we pray, the Holy Spirit helps us to pray the way Jesus taught us. We tell God our Father what is in our thoughts and in our hearts. We ask the Holy Spirit to teach us and help us to live as children of God.

 *Write a short prayer to the Holy Spirit. Use your own words.*

## Praying to the Holy Spirit

Come, Holy Spirit, help me to

_____ .

Come, Holy Spirit, teach me to

_____ .

# Our Church Makes a Difference

## The Work of the Church

Saint Peter and the other disciples received the gift of the Holy Spirit on Pentecost. The work of the Church began. Each year the Church celebrates Pentecost. We sing special songs and say special prayers. The vestments at Mass are red. Sometimes red banners hang in our parish churches.

We remember what happened on the first Pentecost. Peter told people from many countries about Jesus. Many people became followers of Jesus. This was the beginning of the Church.

 *How do you see the people of your parish telling others about Jesus?*

## Our Catholic Faith

### Celebrations of the Church

The Church celebrates the solemnity of Pentecost each year. The most important of the Church's celebrations are called solemnities. Easter is the greatest solemnity of the Church. Other days are called feasts or memorials.

I AM WITH YOU ALWAYS

# What Difference Does Faith Make in My Life?

The Holy Spirit gives you special gifts called talents. These gifts help you to know God's love. They help you to share the gift of God's love with people.

*A flame of fire is one symbol the Church uses for the Holy Spirit. In the flame, write or draw one talent you have. Use that talent to share the gift of God's love with others.*

## Sharing the Gift of God's Love

## My Faith Choice

This week I will share the gift of God's love with other people. I will

_____

_____ .

### Prayer to the Holy Spirit

*The Holy Spirit teaches us to pray and to live as children of God. Pray this prayer to the Holy Spirit together.*

**Leader:** Let us pray to the Holy Spirit.

**Group 1:** Come, Holy Spirit, fill the hearts of your faithful,

**Group 2:** and kindle in them the fire of your love.

**Group 1:** Send forth your Spirit and they shall be created.

**Group 2:** And you will renew the face of the earth. Amen.

## We Remember

*Match each word with its correct meaning.*

**Words**

___ **1.** Pentecost

___ **2.** Ascension

___ **3.** Jesus

___ **4.** Holy Spirit

**Meanings**

**a.** the One who asked the Father to send the Holy Spirit

**b.** the day the work of the Church began

**c.** the third Person of the Holy Trinity

**d.** the return of the Risen Jesus to his Father in heaven

### To Help You Remember

1. Before he returned to his Father in heaven, Jesus promised that the Father would send the Holy Spirit.

2. The Holy Spirit came to the disciples on Pentecost.

3. The Holy Spirit is our helper and teacher.

# With My Family

## This Week . . .

In chapter 9, "The Holy Spirit," your child learned about the Holy Spirit, the third Person of the Holy Trinity. The Father and Jesus sent us the Holy Spirit to be our helper and teacher. The Holy Spirit is the source of all the Church does. The Holy Spirit helps the whole Church learn what Jesus taught. The Holy Spirit helps all the baptized to pray and to live as children of God and followers of Christ.

**For more** on the teaching of the Catholic Church on the mystery of the Holy Spirit, see *Catechism of the Catholic Church* paragraph numbers 687–741.

## Sharing God's Word

Read the Bible story in Acts 2:1–11, 22 about Pentecost or read the adaptation of the story on page 79. Emphasize that the Holy Spirit came to the disciples on Pentecost.

## Praying

In this chapter your child prayed to the Holy Spirit. Read and pray together the prayer on page 83.

## Making a Difference

Choose one of the following activities to do as a family or design a similar activity of your own.

- The Holy Spirit is our helper. Talk about ways you can help one another. Have each family member choose one thing they will do this week to be a helper.

- Make a banner with the words "Come, Holy Spirit." Decorate the banner and display it where it can remind everyone that the Holy Spirit is always with you as your helper.

- Use the prayer to the Holy Spirit on page 83 as your family prayer before meals or bedtime this week. Talk about how your family can call on the Holy Spirit to help your family grow as a Christian family.

For more ideas on ways your family can live your faith, visit the "Faith First for Families" page at **www.FaithFirst.com**. This week take the time to read an article from "Just for Parents."

# We Celebrate Baptism and Confirmation

## 12

## We Pray

LORD, you are the fountain of life.
Based on Psalm 36:10

**Praise to you, almighty God. You created water to give us life. Amen.**

*Why is it a happy time for a family to welcome a new baby?*

When someone is baptized, the person becomes a member of the Church. It is a happy day for our Church family.

*What do you see and hear at Baptism?*

# Baptism and Confirmation

Priest blessing water to be used for Baptism

## Faith Focus

What happens at Baptism and Confirmation?

## Faith Words

**Baptism**
Baptism is the sacrament that joins us to Christ and makes us members of the Church. We receive the gift of the Holy Spirit and become adopted sons and daughters of God.

**Confirmation**
Confirmation is the sacrament in which the gift of the Holy Spirit strengthens us to live our Baptism.

## Baptism

Celebrating Baptism, Confirmation, and Eucharist joins us to Christ and makes us members of the Church. These three sacraments are called Sacraments of Christian Initiation.

**Baptism** is the first sacrament we celebrate. It often takes place during the celebration of Mass. Through Baptism we are joined to Christ and given the gift of the Holy Spirit. We become adopted sons and daughters of God. We are called to live a holy life. We are to love God and our neighbor as Jesus taught.

Dear God,
When I was baptized I received the
Holy Spirit . I became
a member of the Church .
Help me always to follow your
Son, Jesus . Amen.

**ACTIVITY** *Finish this prayer. Pray it quietly in your heart.*

## Celebrating Baptism

We celebrate Baptism with words and actions. We are dipped into the water or water is poured over our head three times. The priest or deacon prays, "I baptize you in the name of the Father, and of the Son, and of the Holy Spirit."

Next the priest or deacon anoints, or blesses, the top of our head with blessed oil. We are then dressed in a white garment. We receive a lighted candle.

The words and actions of Baptism show that we share in God's life. We are to live holy lives and be lights in the world as Jesus was.

 *Look at the pictures on this page. What is happening at Baptism?*

## Celebrating Confirmation

We celebrate the sacrament of **Confirmation** after we are baptized. The bishop usually leads the celebration of Confirmation. During the celebration he prays over us, "Send your Holy Spirit upon them to be their Helper and Guide."

Then the bishop places his right hand on top of our head. He signs our forehead with the blessed oil called holy chrism as he prays, "Be sealed with the gift of the Holy Spirit." We say, "Amen." The bishop then shares a sign of peace with us, saying, "Peace be with you." We answer, "And also with you."

In Confirmation the Holy Spirit strengthens us to live our Baptism. The Holy Spirit helps us to remember and share God's love with others.

```
      O
S P I R I T
      L
```

**ACTIVITY** *For each letter in the word oil write a word about Confirmation.*

# Our Church Makes a Difference

## Fiesta Grande

The children of Saint John Neumann Parish share God's love in a special way. They take part in celebrating Fiesta Grande. Fiesta Grande is a music program performed during Lent.

The parish children dress and decorate individual paper dolls in outfits worn by the people of Central America. These dolls represent the children the people of the parish are helping.

The children also save enough pennies, nickels, dimes, and quarters to sponsor the children. The children write to the children they sponsor and receive messages back. The children also pray for the children they sponsor.

 **QUESTION** *What is one way you and your friends can live your faith in Jesus? How does that share God's love with people?*

## Our Catholic Faith

### Baptismal Candle

At Baptism we receive a lighted candle. The baptismal candle is lighted from the Easter candle. We are given the lighted baptismal candle to remind us that we are to live our faith.

# What Difference Does Faith Make in My Life?

Every time you live your faith in Jesus you show your love for God. The Holy Spirit helps you to live a holy life. You make a difference when you live a holy life.

*On the pathway write three things you can do to live a holy life.*

## Ways to Be Holy

_____

_____

_____

## My Faith Choice

This week I will try to live a holy life. I will

_____

_____ .

# The Forgiving Father
## A Scripture Story

## 13

## We Pray

God always
forgives us.
Based on Psalm 130:4, 7

**God our loving
Father, send us
the gift of your
peace. Amen.**

*What do you say
when someone
says, "Forgive me"?*

Sometimes we
have to ask for
forgiveness. Other
times, we forgive
someone who asks
us to forgive them.
Jesus told many
stories about
forgiveness.

*What Bible story do
you know about
forgiveness?*

# Bible Background

## Faith Focus

What does the parable of the Forgiving Father teach us?

## Faith Words

**parable**
A parable is a story that compares two things. Jesus told parables to help people know and love God better.

## Jesus, the Teacher

Jesus' disciples called him "Teacher." In Jesus' times, this was a great honor and a sign of respect. As other teachers did, Jesus often used stories to teach.

One kind of story told by teachers living in Jesus' time is called a **parable.** In a parable the teacher compares two things. The teacher uses one thing his listeners know well to help them to understand the main point of the story.

The parables Jesus told helped his listeners to know and love God better. These parables also tell us how much God loves us.

 *Think of a favorite Bible story. On the lines write one thing the story teaches you.*

# Reading the Word of God

## The Forgiving Father

One day Jesus told the parable of the Forgiving Father. This parable is about a father who had two sons. Jesus said,

"The younger son asked his father for his share of the family's money because he wanted to leave home. The father gave the son what he asked for. The son left home and soon wasted all his money and became very hungry. The son was sorry for what he had done. The son decided to return to his father.

"The father saw his son walking toward him. He ran to his son, hugged him, and kissed him. Then the son said to him, 'Father, I am very sorry.' The father was very happy his son had come home. He gave a big party to celebrate his son's return."

Based on Luke 15:12–13, 16–18, 20–24

The father was happy and his heart was filled with joy.

 *What do you think Jesus was teaching about God in this parable?*

## God Always Forgives Us

In the parable of the Forgiving Father, Jesus taught about God's mercy and love. God is a loving and forgiving Father.

Sometimes we choose to make wrong choices. Sometimes we sin. As the son did, we realize what we have done is wrong. We are sorry and we ask God for forgiveness. God forgives us and welcomes us with open arms. God is so happy that he rejoices!

 *Write or draw about one way people ask for forgiveness and one way they give forgiveness.*

| Ask for Forgiveness | Give Forgiveness |
|---|---|
|  |  |

# Our Church Makes a Difference

## Saint John Vianney

Saint John Vianney was a special sign of God's forgiveness. John Vianney was a priest. He was honored and respected because of his kindness to people who were sorry for their sins.

There is a story that a special railroad track was built to the village where Father John Vianney lived. The railroad track was built because so many people from all over France wanted to come to John Vianney to celebrate the sacrament of Reconciliation. John Vianney was named a saint in 1925. He is the patron saint of parish priests.

*When have you been kind to someone who asked you to forgive them?*

### Our Catholic Faith

**Act of Contrition**

We ask God for forgiveness in many ways. We celebrate the sacrament of Reconciliation. We pray the Act of Contrition. In the Act of Contrition we tell God we are sorry for our sins and ask for forgiveness.

# What Difference Does Faith Make in My Life?

The Holy Spirit helps us to ask for forgiveness. He also teaches us to forgive others.

*Draw a picture of how you might look when you need to be forgiven. Then draw a picture of how you might look after you have been forgiven.*

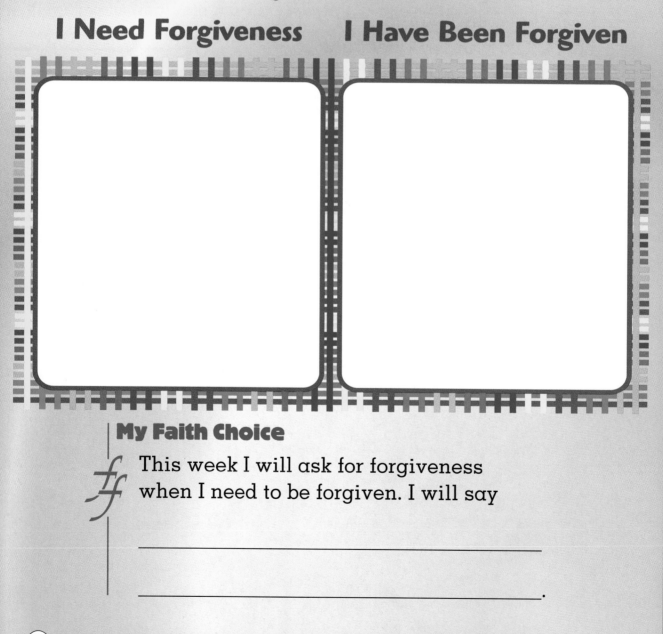

| I Need Forgiveness | I Have Been Forgiven |
|---|---|

## My Faith Choice

This week I will ask for forgiveness when I need to be forgiven. I will say

_____

_____.

# God's Forgiving Love

## 14

## We Pray

Forgive me, O God, because of your goodness.
Based on Psalm 51:3

**All-holy Father, help us to share your forgiving love with others. Amen.**

*What happens when we make a bad choice?*

Sometimes we do something wrong by accident. At other times we may do something wrong on purpose that is against what God wants us to do.

*What happens when we make choices we know are against what God wants us to do?*

# God Always Forgives Us

## Faith Focus

What happens in the sacrament of Reconciliation?

## Faith Words

sin
> Sin is freely choosing to do or say something we know God does not want us to do or say.

Reconciliation
> Reconciliation is a sacrament that brings God's gifts of mercy and forgiving love into our lives.

## We Make Choices

Each day we make many choices. We make good choices. We make bad choices. Some of our bad choices are sins.

We **sin** when we choose to do or say something that we know God does not want us to do or say. We also sin when we choose not to do something we know God wants us to do.

Sin always harms our friendship with God and with other people.

 *Choose one of the photos on this page. On the lines write what you think the child in the photo that you chose is saying.*

_____

_____

_____

## We Need Forgiveness

We need to ask for forgiveness when we sin. The Holy Spirit helps us to turn to God and other people and say, "I am sorry. Please forgive me." We also need to make things better when we sin. This shows we are truly sorry for our sins.

Jesus gave us the sacrament of **Reconciliation**. In this sacrament we tell God we are sorry for our sins. We ask for and receive God's forgiveness. We are forgiven the sins we commit after we are baptized. We receive God's help, or grace, to make good choices to live as children of God. Reconciliation is also called the sacrament of Penance. It is also called Confession.

 *God forgives us when we say we are sorry for our sins. Practice signing "I am sorry."*

I

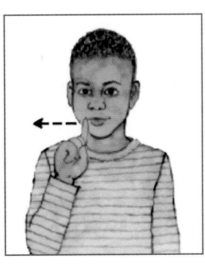

am

sorry.

## We Celebrate Reconciliation

We can celebrate Reconciliation by meeting with the priest by ourselves. Or we can gather with other members of our parish and then meet with the priest. There are four things that are part of every celebration of Reconciliation.

1. **Confession.** We meet with the priest by ourselves and tell him our sins.

2. **Contrition.** We tell God we are truly sorry for our sins. We pray an act of contrition.

3. **Penance.** We are given a penance. Doing our penance helps repair, or heal, the harm we have caused by our sins.

4. **Absolution.** The priest lays his hands on or over our head. We receive God's forgiveness from our sins through the words and actions of the priest.

**ACTIVITY** *Look at the picture at the top of this page. Under the picture write the name of the part of Reconciliation that is shown.*

In Reconciliation we share in God's mercy and forgiving love. We receive the gift of peace. We are reconciled with God and with the Church.

## Saint Dominic Savio

Dominic Savio was a peacemaker. He once said, "I cannot do big things, but I want to do everything, even the small things, for God." Here is a story of one thing Dominic did when he was a teenager.

One day Dominic Savio saw two angry-looking boys holding stones in their hands. Dominic asked, "Why are you holding those stones? You are not going to fight, are you?"

"Before you fight," Dominic told the boys, "think of Jesus. Think of how much people hurt him, and how he forgave them." The boys were ashamed that they were going to fight and dropped the stones.

Dominic was a peacemaker, and the boys became friends again. The Church celebrates the feast day of Saint Dominic Savio on March 9.

 *What is one way to solve problems without fighting?*

### Our Catholic Faith

**The Gift of Peace**

Peace is a gift of God. At the end of the celebration of Reconciliation, we hear words such as "The Lord has freed you from your sins. Go in peace." Christians are to be peacemakers. We are to share the gift of peace we receive from God with others.

# What Difference Does Faith Make in My Life?

In the sacrament of Reconciliation, God forgives you and gives you the gift of peace. You need to forgive others too. When you forgive others, you are a peacemaker.

*Fill in the empty spaces. Describe how you can be a peacemaker.*

## Sharing God's Gift of Peace

I will ask the Holy Spirit to help me live as a peacemaker.

I will forgive my sister, brother, or friend.

I will show my forgiveness by saying

_____.

I will show my forgiveness by doing

_____.

## My Faith Choice

This week I will forgive others. I will do what I have written on the lines above.

# We Gather for Mass

## 15

## We Pray

It is good to give
praise to God!
Based on Psalm 147:1

**God our Father,
we worship you.
We give you
thanks. We
praise you for
your glory.**
**Amen.**

*When do families
gather to celebrate?*

Families gather to
celebrate birthdays,
holidays, and other
special days. All
over the world
Catholics gather
to celebrate Mass.

*What do you see
and hear at Mass?*

# The Mass

## Faith Focus

What happens when we celebrate the Liturgy of the Word?

## Faith Words

**Mass**

The Mass is the most important celebration of the Church. At Mass we worship God. We listen to God's word. We celebrate and share in the Eucharist.

**Liturgy of the Word**

The Liturgy of the Word is the first main part of the Mass. God speaks to us through the readings from the Bible.

## The Introductory Rites

The **Mass** is the most important celebration of the Church. Only a priest or bishop can lead us in the celebration of Mass. He wears special clothes called vestments. At Mass we praise and thank God for all he has done, especially in Jesus. We listen to God's word. We celebrate and share in the Eucharist.

The Mass begins with the Introductory Rites. We stand and sing a hymn as the priest and other ministers enter the church in procession. After we sing the hymn, we pray the Sign of the Cross. The priest greets us, saying, "The Lord be with you." We respond, "And also with you." These words remind us that God is with us. The priest leads us in praying the Collect, or the opening prayer. We respond, "Amen."

 *Describe what is happening in the picture at the top of the page.*

130

# The Liturgy of the Word

After the Introductory Rites, we celebrate the **Liturgy of the Word.** We listen and respond to God's word.

## The Readings from the Bible

At Mass on Sundays and on Saturday evenings we listen to three readings. We sit for the first two readings. The first reading is usually from the Old Testament. After this reading, we sing or pray the responsorial psalm. The second reading is from the New Testament. At the end of both the first and the second readings, the reader says, "The word of the Lord." We respond, "Thanks be to God."

The third reading is from one of the four Gospels. On most days we get ready to listen to the Gospel by standing and singing "Alleluia." The deacon or priest proclaims the Gospel. When he is finished, he says, "The gospel of the Lord." We respond, "Praise to you, Lord Jesus Christ."

 *Underline the responses on pages 130 and 131. Learn them by heart. This will help you to take part in the Mass.*

**Faith-Filled People**

### The Assembly

The assembly is the people who gather to celebrate Mass. All members of the assembly share in the celebration of Mass.

## The Homily

After the Gospel is read, we sit. The priest or deacon helps us to understand the readings. This is called the homily.

## The Profession of Faith

After the homily, we stand. Together we pray aloud a profession of faith, or a creed of the Church. We profess our faith in God the Father, God the Son, and God the Holy Spirit.

## The Prayer of the Faithful

The last part of the Liturgy of the Word is the Prayer of the Faithful. We ask God to help the Church and our country. We pray for other people and for ourselves.

 *Number the parts of the Liturgy of the Word in the correct order.*

_6_ Profession of Faith          _1_ Old Testament Reading

_7_ Prayer of the Faithful       _3_ New Testament Reading

_5_ Homily

_2_ Responsorial Psalm           _4_ Gospel Reading

## Processions at Mass

Processions are prayers in action. A procession is people prayerfully walking together. Processions help us to take part in the celebration of the Mass. There are five processions at Mass.

1. The entrance procession at the beginning of Mass

2. The Gospel procession during the Liturgy of the Word

3. The procession bringing up the gifts to the altar at the beginning of the Liturgy of the Eucharist

4. The procession to receive Holy Communion

5. The procession at the end of Mass

Processions help us remember that we are on a journey. We are on the journey to the kingdom of heaven.

 **QUESTION** *What processions do you take part in during Mass?*

### Our Catholic Faith

**Sanctuary**

The sanctuary is the place in the church where you see the altar and the ambo. The word *sanctuary* means "holy place." The ambo is the stand at which the readers, the deacon, and the priest proclaim the word of God.

# What Difference Does Faith Make in My Life?

You take part in the celebration of Mass in many ways. During the Liturgy of the Word you listen and respond to the word of God.

*Draw or write about a Bible story you heard at Mass. Write the title of your story on the line. Share what the story tells you about God's love.*

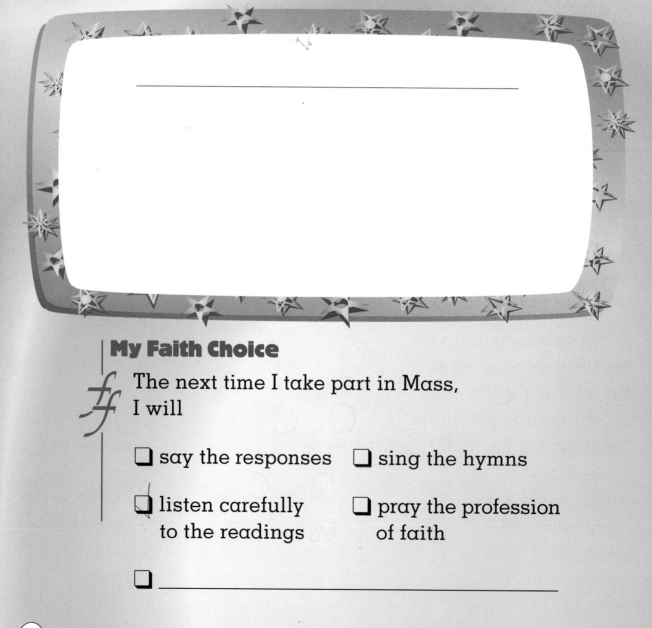

_____

## My Faith Choice

The next time I take part in Mass, I will

- ☐ say the responses
- ☐ sing the hymns
- ☐ listen carefully to the readings
- ☐ pray the profession of faith
- ☐ _____

# The Last Supper

## A Scripture Story

## We Pray

Praise God. . . .
Give praise for his
mighty deeds.
Psalm 150:1–2

**Let us give
thanks to the
Lord our God.
Amen.**

*What kinds of
stories does your
family share
at family meals?*

Jesus shared many
meals with his
disciples. At one
special meal each
year, they shared
the story of God's
love for his people.

*What do you know
about the last meal
Jesus shared with
his disciples?*

The chalice, bread, and
grapes—symbols for
the Eucharist

137

# Bible Background

## Faith Focus

Why is the Last Supper important for Christians?

## Faith Words

**Last Supper**
The Last Supper is the special meal that Jesus ate with his disciples on the night before he died.

## Jesus Celebrates Passover

Passover is a holy time of the year for the Jewish people. Jesus belonged to the Jewish people. In the Old Testament the Jewish people are also called the Israelites. During Passover the Jewish people gather for a special meal. They bless and thank God for everything he has done and does for them.

Jesus ate this special meal with his disciples on the night before he died. This meal was the last meal Jesus and his disciples ate together. Christians call this meal the **Last Supper.**

 Circle the first letter and every other letter. Discover what Jesus and the disciples did at the Last Supper.

T o H B E R Y c B P L Z E
T S R S o E B D Z A F N I
D W T C H L A S N T K V E
F D J G U o S D.

They bless ed
_____ .

138

# Reading the Word of God

## The Last Supper

Jesus and his disciples shared the Last Supper in the city of Jerusalem. Jerusalem is the most important city of the Jewish people. Read what happened at the Last Supper.

During the meal Jesus took bread into his hands and said a blessing prayer. He broke the bread into pieces. Giving the bread to his disciples, Jesus said, "Take this. It is my body. Do this in memory of me."

Jesus took a cup of wine and gave thanks to God. Giving the cup of wine to his disciples, he said, "Drink it." They all drank from the cup. Jesus said, "This is my blood, which is poured out for many."          Based on Luke 22:17–20

 When does the Church gather to do what Jesus asked us to do at the Last Supper?

## We Gather Around the Altar

Jesus gathered around a table with his disciples to celebrate the Last Supper. We gather around the altar to celebrate the Eucharist. Another name for the altar is the Table of the Lord.

At the Eucharist the Church does what Jesus did at the Last Supper. The priest takes bread and wine. Through the words of the priest and the power of the Holy Spirit, the bread and wine become the Body and Blood of Christ. We receive the Body and Blood of Christ in Holy Communion.

**ACTIVITY** *Color the stained-glass window. Color the Xs white and Os yellow. Use other colors for the other spaces. On the line write a title for your window.*

# Our Church Makes a Difference

## The Saint Francis Breadline

At the Last Supper, Jesus told his disciples to love and serve one another as he did. The Franciscans in New York City follow Jesus' command. Franciscans are followers of Saint Francis of Assisi.

People in New York City who need food or clothing come to the Church of Saint Francis of Assisi. The Franciscans are there every morning to greet them.

The Franciscans give each person sandwiches and something to drink. Most importantly, the Franciscans share a smile and words of welcome. They share the love and respect Saint Francis of Assisi himself shared with everyone he met.

QUESTION *What ways can you and your family serve people as Jesus told us to do?*

# What Difference Does Faith Make in My Life?

At Mass you receive the gift of the Body and Blood of Christ. One way you can thank God for the blessings he gives you is by sharing your blessings with other people.

*Write a prayer of thanks to God for all his blessings. Ask the Holy Spirit to help you share your blessings with others.*

## THANK YOU, GOD

## My Faith Choice

This week I will share the blessings God has given me. I will

_____

_____.

## We Pray

### Blessed Be God

*Blessing prayers tell God we believe that all our blessings come from him. Learn the response "Blessed be God for ever." Learn the words by heart. Pray them in this prayer.*

**Leader:**  God our Father, we thank you for all your blessings.

**All:**  **Blessed be God for ever.**

**Leader:**  Thank you, God, for

_____ .

**All:**  **Blessed be God for ever.**

## We Remember

*Use the code to discover Jesus' words at the Last Supper.*

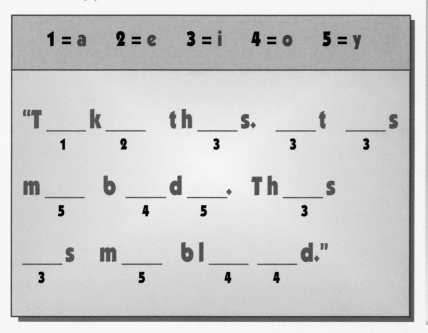

1 = a   2 = e   3 = i   4 = o   5 = y

"T__k__ th__s. __t __s
   1    2      3     3    3

m__ b__d__. Th__s
  5    4   5       3

__s m__ bl__ __d."
 3    5     4   4

### To Help You Remember

1. Jesus ate the Last Supper with his disciples on the night before he died.

2. At the Last Supper Jesus gave his followers his Body and Blood.

3. At Mass we gather around the altar and do what Jesus did at the Last Supper.

**Grade 2 • Chapter 16**  143

## This Week . . .

In chapter 16, "The Last Supper: A Scripture Story," your child learned about the Last Supper and the connection between the Last Supper and the Eucharist. At the Last Supper Jesus took the bread and gave it to his disciples, saying, "This is my body." He took the cup of wine and gave it to his disciples, saying, "This is my blood." Then he said, "Do this in memory of me." At the celebration of the Eucharist, the Church does what Jesus asked. We celebrate what happened at the Last Supper. Through the power of the Holy Spirit and the words of the priest, the bread and wine become the Body and Blood of Christ. Jesus is really and truly present under the appearances of bread and wine.

**For more** on the teachings of the Catholic Church on the Last Supper and the Eucharist, see *Catechism of the Catholic Church* paragraph numbers 1333–1344.

## Sharing God's Word

Read together the Bible story in Luke 22:14–20 about the Last Supper or read the adaptation of the story on page 139. Emphasize that at the Last Supper Jesus instituted, or gave, the Church the Eucharist.

## Praying

In this chapter your child prayed a blessing prayer, using a response from the Mass. Read and pray together the blessing prayer on page 143.

## Making a Difference

Choose one of the following activities to do as a family or design a similar activity of your own.

• After your family takes part in Mass this week, take time to visit your parish tabernacle. The tabernacle is where the consecrated bread, or Blessed Sacrament, is kept.

• This week at Mass remind your child that what Jesus did at the Last Supper is part of the Eucharistic Prayer. After Mass talk with your child about the Last Supper and the Mass.

• The Eucharist strengthens us to love and serve others as Jesus commanded his followers to do. Choose one thing your family can do this week to live as followers of Jesus.

For more ideas on ways your family can live your faith, visit the "Faith First for Families" page at **www.FaithFirst.com**. Click on "Questions Kids Ask." Help your child grow in faith.

# We Give Thanks to God

## We Pray

It is good to give
thanks to the LORD.

Psalm 92:2

**Father, always
and everywhere
we give you
thanks through
Jesus Christ,
your Son.**

**Amen.**

*What is a gift you
have received?*

When we receive
a gift, we say,
"Thank you." At
Mass we thank
God for Jesus and
for everything he
did for us.

*What are you
thankful to God for?*

# Give Thanks and Praise to God

## Faith Focus

What happens when we celebrate the Liturgy of the Eucharist?

## Faith Words

**Eucharist**
The Eucharist is the sacrament of the Body and Blood of Jesus Christ.

**Liturgy of the Eucharist**
The Liturgy of the Eucharist is the second main part of the Mass. The Church does what Jesus did at the Last Supper.

## The Liturgy of the Eucharist

The **Liturgy of the Eucharist** is the second main part of the Mass. The word *eucharist* means "to give thanks."

### The Preparation of the Gifts

The Liturgy of the Eucharist begins with the preparation of the gifts. Members of the assembly bring our gifts of bread and wine to the altar. The priest tells God all our blessings come from him. We respond, "Blessed be God for ever." The priest then leads us in the Prayer over the Offerings. We respond, "Amen."

*Think of the blessings God has given you and your family. Pray with your class, "Blessed be God for ever."*

## The Eucharistic Prayer

The Eucharistic Prayer is the Church's great prayer of thanksgiving. During this prayer the Church does what Jesus did at the Last Supper.

The priest holds the bread in his hands and says,
"Take this, all of you, and eat it: this is my body which will be given up for you."

Then the priest holds up the chalice of wine and says,
"Take this, all of you, and drink from it: this is the cup of my blood, the blood of the new and everlasting covenant. It will be shed for you and for all so that sins may be forgiven. Do this in memory of me."

The bread and wine become Jesus' Body and Blood through the power of the Holy Spirit and the words of the priest. What looks like bread and wine is no longer bread and wine. It is really Jesus. At the end of the Eucharistic Prayer the assembly stands and sings "Amen."

**ACTIVITY**

Amen means "It is true." Color the letters in the word Amen. Think of what happens at Mass and pray "Amen."

AMEN

## Communion

We walk in procession to receive the consecrated bread at the altar. The Eucharist is offered to us with the words "The body of Christ." We bow our heads to honor Jesus present in the sacrament and respond, "Amen." We receive and eat the consecrated bread.

If we receive from the cup, the cup of consecrated wine is offered to us. We hear the words "The blood of Christ." We bow our heads and respond, "Amen." We take the cup and drink from it.

We receive strength to live as followers of Jesus. We become closer to Jesus, Mary, the saints, and all the members of the Church. We receive Jesus' promise, or pledge, that we too will live forever in heaven.

 *On each note card write one way you live as a follower of Jesus.*

# Our Church Makes a Difference

## Love and Serve the Lord

The celebration of Mass ends with the Concluding Rites. We receive God's blessing. The deacon or priest sends us forth using these or similar words, "Go in peace to love and serve the Lord." We respond, "Thanks be to God."

We show our thanks to God when we try our best to live as Jesus taught. We try to love one another. We do things that are difficult to do because of our love for God and for others. When we do this, we love God and people as Jesus did.

### Our Catholic Faith

**The Holy Sacrifice**

Jesus' sacrifice on the cross is the greatest act of love for God the Father and for all people. The Mass is also called the Holy Sacrifice. At Mass we share in the sacrifice of Jesus. We join with Jesus and show our love for God. We receive God's grace to love one another as Jesus commanded us to do.

*These children have chosen ways to live as Jesus taught. What is one way you can live as Jesus taught?*

# What Difference Does Faith Make in My Life?

When you share in the Eucharist, you receive the grace to live as a follower of Jesus.

*On each door write one reason Catholics celebrate Mass.*

## Celebrating Mass

## My Faith Choice

I will show my thanks to God this week for the gift of the Eucharist. I will

_____

_____.

Name _____

## A. The Best Word

*Complete the sentences. Color the circle next to the best choice for each sentence.*

1. The seven ___ are signs of God's love for us.

   ○ Bibles    ○ sacraments    ○ prayers

2. Water and oil are used in the sacrament of ___.

   ○ Baptism    ○ Reconciliation    ○ Matrimony

3. Jesus told the parable of the Forgiving ___ to teach us about God's forgiveness.

   ○ Son    ○ Father    ○ Brother

4. In the sacrament of ___ we receive God's forgiveness for our sins.

   ○ Matrimony    ○ Reconciliation    ○ Confirmation

5. The ___ is the most important celebration of the Church.

   ○ Mass    ○ rosary    ○ Nativity

## B. Sacraments

Draw a line to connect the clues to the correct sacrament.

| Sacrament | Clue |
|---|---|
| 1. Baptism | a. strengthened by the Holy Spirit |
| 2. Confirmation | b. forgiveness of sins committed after Baptism |
| 3. Eucharist | c. first sacrament we receive |
| 4. Reconciliation | d. Body and Blood of Christ |

## C. What I Have Learned

1. Name two things you learned in this unit. Tell a partner.

_____

_____

2. Look at the faith words listed on page 96. Circle the ones that you know now.

## D. From a Scripture Story

Draw two pictures about the parable of the Forgiving Father. Tell the beginning and the end of the parable. Give a title to each picture.

# Unit 3 • We Live

*What are some ways we live the Ten Commandments?*

# Getting Ready

## What I Have Learned

*What is something you already know about these faith words?*

The Ten Commandments

_____

_____

Your conscience

_____

_____

## Words to Know

*Put an X next to the faith words you know. Put a ? next to words you need to know more about.*

**Faith Words**

_____ grace

_____ Great Commandment

_____ conscience

_____ heaven

_____ sanctifying grace

## A Question I Have

*What question would you like to ask about the Great Commandment?*

_____

_____

_____

## A Scripture Story

Jesus teaching the Great Commandment

*What is the Great Commandment?*

# We Are God's Children

## We Pray

I love you, LORD.
Psalm 18:2

**Blessed be Jesus, whom you sent to be the friend of children.**
**Amen.**

*Who loves you?*

Knowing people love us makes us feel good inside. God loves us more than anyone. We are children of God.

*What do you think it means to be a child of God?*

# We Are Children of God

## Faith Focus

What do we do to live as children of God?

## Faith Words

**honor**
To honor someone is to treat them with kindness, respect, and love.

**grace**
Grace is the gift of God sharing his life with us. It is also God helping us to make good choices to live as children of God.

Imagine you are one of the children in the picture. What would you say to Jesus?

## Jesus and the Children

The Bible teaches that God gives every person a great **honor.** He creates every person in his image and likeness. God shares his life with us. He creates us to be children of God.

Jesus taught us to honor God, ourselves, and other people. He taught us to treat people with kindness, respect, and love. He taught us to honor all people as children of God.

Detail from
*Christ with the Children*
by American artist
Shannon Stirnweis

## Jesus Is Our Teacher

The disciples of Jesus honored him in many ways. They honored and respected him as a teacher. In Jesus' time to call someone "Teacher" was a sign of great honor and respect.

Jesus' disciples carefully listened to him. They learned from him. He told them this about himself. He said,

"I am the way, the truth, and the life. I will lead you to God."

Based on John 14:6

Jesus is our teacher. We listen to him. We try our best to live as he taught.

**Faith-Filled People**

### Teresa of Avila

Saint Teresa of Avila lived in Spain. She was a great teacher of the faith of the Church. The Church honors Saint Teresa of Avila as one of the Doctors of the Church. This means that the Church honors her as a great teacher. The Church celebrates her feast day on October 15.

**ACTIVITY** *Follow each path to Jesus. Ask Jesus to teach you to live as a child of God.*

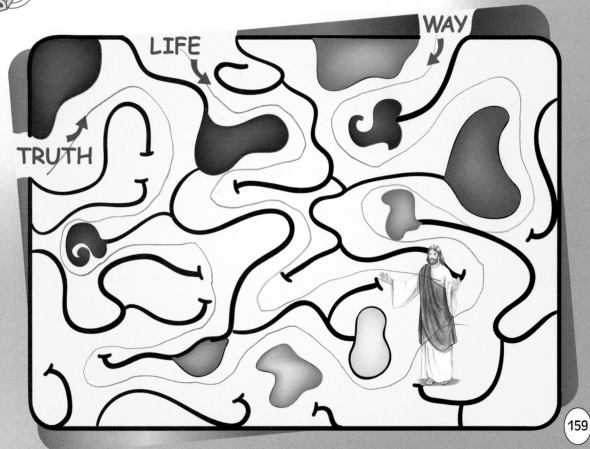

LIFE    WAY

TRUTH

159

## Making Choices

Jesus taught us how to make good choices to live as children of God. When we make good choices, we show that we are proud and honored to call Jesus "Teacher." We show we are trying our best to live as children of God. We love God and other people as Jesus did.

We ask God for the **grace,** or help, to make good choices to live as children of God. The Holy Spirit helps us to make good choices. When we make good choices, we grow as children of God.

*Put a ✔ in the boxes next to the people who help you learn to make good choices to live as a child of God.*

☐ parent     ☐ grandparent

☐ priest     ☐ friend

☐ teacher     ☐ coach

☐ _____
(name of someone else)

# Our Church Makes a Difference

## Saint Thérèse of Lisieux

Saint Thérèse of Lisieux was proud to be a child of God. Thérèse tried her best to do little things well.

Thérèse wrote a story about her life. She wrote about the little things we can do each day out of love. We can say "Thank you," help at home, and care for our things. When we do little things out of love as Saint Thérèse did, we honor and respect God. We honor and respect other people and ourselves. We do what Jesus taught us to do.

Saint Thérèse of Lisieux is also called Saint Thérèse of the Child Jesus. She is also known as The Little Flower. Her feast day is October 1.

**What are some of the little things people do to honor and respect God, themselves, and other people?**

### Our Catholic Faith

**Fruits of the Holy Spirit**

The Bible names some signs that show we are trying our best to live as children of God. Three of these signs are joy, generosity, and kindness. We call these signs fruits of the Holy Spirit.

# What Difference Does Faith Make in My Life?

Each day the Holy Spirit helps you to live as a child of God. The Holy Spirit helps you to make choices that show you are proud to be a child of God.

*Write some words of kindness you say. Then write acts of kindness you do that show you are a child of God.*

## Living as a Child of God

**Say**

_____

_____

_____

**Do**

_____

_____

_____

**My Faith Choice**

This week I will surprise someone with this act of kindness. I will

_____

_____ .

## We Pray

# May God Bless Us

*At the conclusion of Mass the priest asks God to bless the people. Pray this prayer to ask God to bless your class.*

**Leader:** Father, we ask your blessing on us.

**All:** **Father, we are your children.**

**Leader:** Guide us to choose what is good and to do your will.

**All:** **Father, we are your children.**

**Leader:** *As each child comes forward, place a hand on the child's head, saying:* May God bless us and keep us.

**All:** **Amen.**

## We Remember

*Find and circle the words hidden in the puzzle. Use the words to share with a partner how you can live as a child of God.*

| RESPECT | GOOD | LOVE | |
|---|---|---|---|
| FOLLOW | CHOICES | HONOR | FAITH |

```
R E S P E C T L H O Q L T H R A
O F O L L O W P N Z T F A I T H
C H O I C E S T R W L O V E P T
Y H O N O R L I G O O D R W Z A
```

### To Help You Remember

1. All people are to be honored and respected because God has created everyone to be a child of God.

2. Jesus taught that we are to live as children of God.

3. The Holy Spirit helps us to make choices to live as children of God.

## This Week . . .

In chapter 18, "We Are God's Children," your child learned to honor and respect all people. Every person deserves our respect. Every person has the dignity of being a child of God, who is created in the image and likeness of God. Jesus is our Teacher. He showed us how to live as children of God. He said, "I am the way, the truth, and the life. I will lead you to God" (based on John 14:6). We honor and respect Jesus as our Teacher when we try our best to live as he taught. All our words and actions are to show respect for God, other people, and ourselves.

**For more** on the teachings of the Catholic Church on the dignity of the human person, grace, and holiness, see *Catechism of the Catholic Church* paragraph numbers 1699–1756 and 1996–2016.

## Sharing God's Word

Read together the Bible story in Mark 10:13–16 about Jesus and the children. Emphasize that Jesus taught us to respect all people as children of God.

## Praying

In this chapter your child prayed a prayer asking God's blessing on all the members of the class. Pray together the prayer on page 163.

## Making a Difference

Choose one of the following activities to do as a family or design a similar activity of your own.

• Talk about making good choices. Help your child learn how we know that we are making or have made good choices. Discuss how the Church helps us make good choices.

• Saint Thérèse of Lisieux focused on doing the little things in life out of love. Share how your family can live as Saint Thérèse did and do the little things that are part of daily life out of love.

• Share ideas on how acts and words of kindness show we are children of God. Choose and do something this week to live as children of God.

For more ideas on ways your family can live your faith, visit the "Faith First for Families" page at **www.FaithFirst.com**. Click on "Saints" and learn about other faith-filled people of the Church.

# The Great Commandment
## A Scripture Story

**19**

## We Pray

LORD God, your
law brings us joy
and happiness.
Based on Psalm 1:2

**Lord our God,
we love you with
all our heart.
Amen.**

*What new thing
have you learned
this week?*

Watching, listening,
and asking
questions are all
ways of learning.
Jesus helps us to
learn how to live as
children of God.

*What are some
ways you live as
a child of God?*

# Bible Background

## Faith Focus

What does the Great Commandment help us to do?

## Faith Words

**Temple in Jerusalem**
A temple is a building built to honor God. The Jewish people in Jesus' time worshiped God in the Temple in Jerusalem.

**Great Commandment**
The Great Commandment is to love God above all else and to love others as we love ourselves.

## The Temple in Jerusalem

In Jesus' time the Jewish people came to the **Temple in Jerusalem** to worship God. A temple is a building built to honor God. The Temple in Jerusalem was the largest building in the city. It was a beautiful white building with a golden roof.

The people met in the Temple courtyard with the teachers of God's Law. They gathered there to listen to and to learn about God's Law.

 Christians gather in churches to worship God and to learn about God. Draw yourself worshiping God in your parish church.

Drawing of Temple in Jerusalem

# Reading the Word of God

## Jesus Teaches in the Temple

One day Jesus was in the Temple. A teacher of God's Law asked Jesus which commandment of God is the greatest. Jesus gave him this answer.

"You shall love the Lord your God with all your heart, and with all your soul, and with all your mind. This is the first and greatest commandment. The second commandment is like the first one. You shall love your neighbor as yourself. There is no other commandment greater than these two."     Based on Matthew 22:37–40

Jesus named two commandments. Together both commandments make up one **Great Commandment.**

*Read the Scripture verses again. Name the two commandments that make up the Great Commandment.*

# Understanding the Word of God

## The Great Commandment

The first part of the Great Commandment teaches that God is the center of our life. It teaches us to love God above all else.

- We show our love for God when we honor and respect God in all we do and say.
- We show our love for God when we pray.

The second part of the Great Commandment teaches us to treat others as we like to be treated. We are to respect and honor all people.

- We respect and honor all people when we help them care for their things.
- We respect and honor people when we treat them fairly.

**ACTIVITY** *Tell how the people in the pictures are showing love for God and for one another. Draw how you can live the Great Commandment.*

Cut neibors grass

# Our Church Makes a Difference

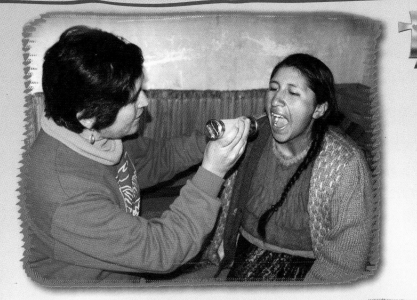

## Our Catholic Faith

**Mission Cross**

Before missionaries travel to the missions, they are blessed and given a cross. The cross reminds them of the love of Jesus for God and for all people.

## Missionaries

Christians live the Great Commandment in many different ways. Missionaries travel to teach others about Jesus. Missionaries are often priests, religious sisters, religious brothers, or laypeople who are married or single. They can be teachers, doctors, nurses, farmers, and scientists.

Christian missionaries live the Great Commandment. They help people come to know and believe in Jesus and God's love for them. They help people to live as Jesus taught and to treat one another with respect.

**QUESTION** How are the missionaries in these pictures living the Great Commandment?

# What Difference Does Faith Make in My Life?

The Holy Spirit helps you to live the Great Commandment.

*Pretend you are teaching a kindergarten class about the Great Commandment. Write or draw what you are telling the class.*

## Sharing with Others

live the by loving god, and helping others

## My Faith Choice

*ff* This week I will live the Great Commandment. I will

pray for my mother

# The Ten Commandments

## 20

## We Pray

LORD God, teach me
your ways.
> Based on Psalm 25:5

**God our Father,
help us to live
your laws.**

> **Amen.**

*Name a rule in
your home that
everyone has to
follow.*

Family rules help
us to love one
another. The Ten
Commandments
are rules God gave
us. They help all
people to live as
children of God.

*Name the
Commandments
you know.*

# Living the Commandments

## Faith Focus

How do the Ten Commandments help people to live holy lives?

## Faith Words

**commandments**
Commandments are rules that help us to live holy lives.

**Ten Commandments**
The Ten Commandments are the laws that God gave Moses that teach us to live as God's people.

## Love God

Commandments are rules. The **commandments** God gives us help us to live holy lives. God gave us the **Ten Commandments.** The first three Commandments teach us to love and respect God.

The First Commandment teaches us that there is only one God. We worship God alone. We love God above all else.

The Second Commandment teaches us that God's name is holy. We speak God's name with reverence. We always speak it with respect and honor.

The Third Commandment teaches us to keep one day each week as God's day. Sunday is that day for Christians. It is the Lord's Day. Each Sunday Catholics gather together and celebrate the Eucharist. We make time to show that God is our Father and we are his children.

**ACTIVITY** *Write one way you can keep one of the first three Commandments.*

_____

_____

## Love Others

The Fourth Commandment teaches us to honor and obey our parents. It also tells us to honor and obey grandparents, teachers, and other people who parents ask to help guide their children.

The Fifth Commandment teaches us to take care of our own lives and the lives of other people. We take care of our health. We do not harm ourselves or other people.

The Sixth Commandment and the Ninth Commandment teach us to respect our own bodies and the bodies of other people. We are not to let people touch us in the wrong way.

*Look at the pictures on this page. Describe how the people are showing love for other people.*

### Faith-Filled People

**John Bosco**

Before he became a priest, Saint John Bosco went to circuses to learn the tricks magicians performed. Younger boys gathered around John Bosco to watch him do the tricks. When they did, John Bosco taught the boys about Jesus by repeating the homily he heard at Mass. The Church celebrates the feast day of Saint John Bosco on January 31.

175

## Three More Commandments

The Seventh Commandment teaches us to respect the property of other people. We do not steal or cheat. When we want to use something that belongs to someone else, we ask permission. We use what we borrow correctly and return it in good condition.

The Eighth Commandment teaches us to be honest and truthful. We do not lie.

The Tenth Commandment teaches us to use food and water and all creation fairly. The good things we have and the things we can do are all gifts from God. We share our gifts. We are not jealous of other people.

When we live the Ten Commandments, we are living as children of God. We are living holy lives.

 *On the lines describe what each picture tells us about living as a child of God.*

# Our Church Makes a Difference

## Saint Vincent de Paul

People who live the Commandments help to build a kind and fair world. They treat people as children of God. They share God's love with people as Jesus did.

Saint Vincent de Paul took care of the sick. He gave clothes and food to the poor. He helped people to find jobs and to build homes.

Today people in many parishes follow the example of Saint Vincent de Paul. They are members of the Saint Vincent de Paul Society.

 **QUESTION** *What do the people of your parish do to show they are building a kind and fair world?*

### ✝ Our Catholic Faith

**Almsgiving**

*Almsgiving* is a word that means "sharing something to help the poor." Jesus told us that when we help the poor and the hungry, we are helping him. From the very beginning of the Church, Christians have always done what Jesus asked. The first Christians did this very well. Their neighbors used to say, "See how much they love one another."

# What Difference Does Faith Make in My Life?

When you live the Ten Commandments, you are living as a child of God. You are living a holy life. You are building a kind and fair world.

*The sentences in the frames name seven ways to live the Ten Commandments. Choose one. Write or draw how you can do what it says.*

## Living the Commandments

Respect your parents.

Take care of yourself.

Go to church. Be kind.

Be generous.

Treat others fairly.

Listen to your grandma and grandpa.

## My Faith Choice

I will keep the _____ Commandment this week. I will

_____

_____ .

## We Pray

### Prayer to the Holy Spirit

*Learn to sign the prayer "Come, Holy Spirit."*
*Pray it quietly alone and pray it with others.*

**Come**　　　　　　　　**Holy Spirit**

## We Remember

*Use the words in the box to complete the sentences.*

┄┄┄┄┄┄┄┄┄┄┄┄┄┄┄┄┄┄┄┄┄
**Ten**　　　**seven**　　　**three**
┄┄┄┄┄┄┄┄┄┄┄┄┄┄┄┄┄┄┄┄┄

1. God gave us the _____ Commandments.

2. The first _____ Commandments tell us ways to love God above all else.

3. The last _____ Commandments tell us ways we are to love others as we love ourselves.

**To Help You Remember**

1. The Ten Commandments teach us to live the Great Commandment.

2. The first three Commandments teach us to love, honor, and respect God.

3. The last seven Commandments teach us to love, honor, and respect other people and ourselves.

## This Week . . .

In chapter 20, "The Ten Commandments," your child learned that the Commandments guide us in living the Great Commandment. The first three Commandments name ways that we are to love, honor, and respect God. The last seven Commandments name ways we are to love, honor, and respect other people, ourselves, and all of God's creation. When we live the Ten Commandments, we live as children of God. We live holy lives. We prepare for the coming of the kingdom of God.

**For more** on the teachings of the Catholic Church on the Ten Commandments, see *Catechism of the Catholic Church* "First Commandment" (2083–2132), "Second Commandment" (2142–2159), "Third Commandment" (2168–2188), "Fourth Commandment" (2196–2246), "Fifth Commandment" (2258–2317), "Sixth Commandment" (2331–2391), "Seventh Commandment" (2401–2449), "Eighth Commandment" (2464–2503), "Ninth Commandment" (2514–2527), and "Tenth Commandment" (2534–2550).

## Sharing God's Word

Read together Exodus 20:1–3, 7–17. Talk about how the Ten Commandments help us to live holy lives. Emphasize that the Ten Commandments are God's laws. They help us to live the Great Commandment.

## Praying

In this chapter your child signed a prayer to the Holy Spirit. Read and pray together the prayer on page 179.

## Making a Difference

Choose one of the following activities to do as a family or design a similar activity of your own.

• Write and illustrate your own storybook about how your family shows respect for God and other people.

• We can show our love for God by setting aside time each day to pray. Make prayer rocks to carry in your pockets. Use them as reminders to set aside time to pray often throughout the day. When you put your hand into your pocket, you will be reminded to pray. You will also be reminded that God is always with you.

• Talk about what your parish does to live the Ten Commandments. You might use a copy of your parish bulletin or visit your parish web site as a guide for your discussion.

For more ideas on ways your family can live your faith, visit the "Faith First for Families" page at **www.FaithFirst.com**. The "Make a Difference" page goes especially well with this chapter.

# Proverbs
## A Scripture Story

**21**

## We Pray

The precepts of
the LORD are right.
*Psalm 19:9*

**Lord God, teach
me to live your
Commandments.
Amen.**

*What sayings do
you know that help
you to remember to
do something?*

The saying "Buckle
Up" helps us to
make a safe choice.
The Bible has many
sayings that help
us to make wise
choices.

*What sayings
from the Bible do
you know?*

# Bible Background

## Faith Focus

What are proverbs?

## Faith Words

**proverbs**
Proverbs are short sayings that help us to make wise choices.

**wise choice**
A wise choice is a choice that helps us to live as children of God.

## Sayings in the Bible

The Bible has many wise sayings. These sayings are called **proverbs.** They help God's people to make **wise choices** to live as children of God.

Many of God's people in Old Testament times could not read or write. Listening very carefully and learning proverbs by heart helped them to make wise choices.

**ACTIVITY** *Think of wise sayings you know. For example, "Buckle Up" or "Stop, Drop, and Roll." Write or draw a picture of another saying you know that helps you to make wise choices.*

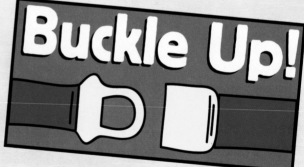

# Reading the Word of God

## The Book of Proverbs

The writers of the Bible collected many proverbs. You can read them in the Book of Proverbs in the Old Testament. Each proverb helps us to love God, other people, and ourselves.

Read these two proverbs. Think about how each can help you to live as a child of God.

Trust God with all your heart.
  Do not think you always have
    the answers.

Based on Proverbs 3:5

Ask God's help before
  you do something.
It is the secret to doing
  the right thing.

Based on Proverbs 16:3

 How does each of these two proverbs help you to live as a child of God?

# Understanding the Word of God

## Living as Children of God

The first proverb on page 183 begins "Trust God with all your heart." Learn it by heart. Following its advice will help you to keep God first in your life. It will help you to love God above all else.

The second proverb teaches us to pray before we make our choices. Praying helps us to make wise choices.

 *Write a second part for this proverb. Share ways that your proverb can help you to live as a child of God.*

### Writing a Proverb

Speak kindly,
　　and you will make peace.
Speak unkindly,
　　and you will

_____

_____

WE ARE ALL CHILDREN OF GOD

# Our Church Makes a Difference

## Christian Sayings

The Church has always had people to help us to live as followers of Christ. Many of these people said things that are like proverbs.

Saint Ignatius of Loyola once said, "See God in all things." What a wonderful way to help us to remember that God is always with us. What a wonderful way to remember to love God above all else with our whole heart.

**QUESTION** *Who are some of the people who give you good advice? What good advice do they give you? How does that advice help you to love God with your whole heart?*

### Our Catholic Faith

**The Bishop's Motto**

A motto is another kind of short saying. Bishops use a motto to describe their work as a bishop. Pope John Paul II showed his love for Mary by choosing the motto "I Am Completely Yours, Mary."

# See God in All Things

# What Difference Does Faith Make in My Life?

What sayings do you know that help you to make wise choices? The Holy Spirit will help you to use these sayings to live as a follower of Jesus Christ.

*Think about some of the good advice your parents or teachers have given you to live as a child of God. Write or draw the actions that show you are following that advice.*

## Wise Choices

## My Faith Choice

 This week when I need help making a choice to live as a child of God, I will ask someone for help. I will ask

_____.

## We Pray to the Lord

*At Baptism we receive the grace to live the Commandments as Jesus taught. Pray this prayer. Tell God you will try your best to live as a follower of Jesus.*

**Leader:** Remember the Lord's teachings. Keep his laws with all your heart.

**All:** **Lord, teach us your laws.**

**Leader:** Trust in the Lord with all your heart. The Lord will lead you on a straight path.

**All:** **We will trust the Lord always.**

Based on Psalm 119:33–34

## We Remember

*Circle Yes if you agree with a sentence. Circle No if you do not agree with a sentence.*

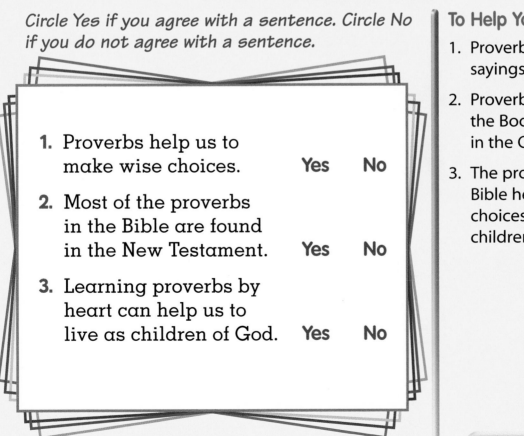

1. Proverbs help us to make wise choices.     **Yes     No**

2. Most of the proverbs in the Bible are found in the New Testament.     **Yes     No**

3. Learning proverbs by heart can help us to live as children of God.     **Yes     No**

### To Help You Remember

1. Proverbs are wise sayings.

2. Proverbs are found in the Book of Proverbs in the Old Testament.

3. The proverbs in the Bible help us to make choices to live as children of God.

## This Week . . .

In chapter 21, "Proverbs: A Scripture Story," your child learned about proverbs, in particular the proverbs found in Sacred Scripture. Proverbs in the Bible are short sayings that help us make wise decisions. Wisdom is one of the seven gifts of the Holy Spirit. This gift helps us know the purpose and plan of God and see the world as God sees it. Wisdom and the other gifts of the Holy Spirit help us live our relationship with God and with other people. They guide us to use and respect all of creation according to God's loving plan for creation.

**For more** on the teachings of the Catholic Church on the gifts of the Holy Spirit and the importance of praying the Scriptures, see *Catechism of the Catholic Church* paragraph numbers 1830–1832, 2568–2589, and 2653–2654.

## Sharing God's Word

Read together Proverbs 3:5 and Proverbs 16:3 or read the adaptation of these verses on page 183. Emphasize that the proverbs in the Bible can help us make choices to live as children of God.

## Praying

In this chapter your child prayed a prayer based on verses from Psalm 119. Read and pray together the prayer on page 187.

## Making a Difference

Choose one of the following activities to do as a family or design a similar activity of your own.

- Choose one of the proverbs in this chapter. Tell how the proverb can help your family live as children of God.

- Talk about Gospel sayings your family may use; for example, "God bless you" or "God reward you."

- Share with one another the names of people who give you advice that helps you make wise family decisions. Share what wise advice these people have given you.

For more ideas on ways your family can live your faith, visit the "Faith First for Families" page at **www.FaithFirst.com**. Visit the "Game" site. Ask your child to show you her or his favorite game. Play it together.

# We Make Choices

## We Pray

LORD God, doing
   your will makes
   me happy.
         Based on Psalm 40:9

**We thank you,
God our Father.
You made us to
love you and
one another.
                  Amen.**

*What wise choices
did you make
today?*

We make many
wise choices each
day. Jesus teaches
us how to make
wise choices.

*What can help
you to make wise
choices?*

# We Follow Jesus

## Faith Focus

Why is it important to follow God's will when we make choices?

## Faith Words

**consequences**
Consequences are the good or bad things that happen when we make choices.

**conscience**
Conscience is a gift from God that helps us to make wise choices.

## Wise Choices Bring Happiness

God sent Jesus to show us how to make wise choices. Jesus always did what his Father asked him to do. We will be truly happy when we make choices as Jesus taught us.

God wants us to be happy now and forever in heaven. Heaven is being happy with God and with all the saints forever.

*Look and think about what is happening in these pictures. Tell what choice you would make next. Share why your choices are good choices.*

Choices

## Choosing Right and Wrong

God lets us make choices for ourselves. We can choose to do or not to do God's will. In the Bible we read,

> When God created us, he gave us free choice. It is our choice to do God's will.

Based on Sirach 15:14–15

Things happen when we make choices. These are called **consequences.** We are responsible for the consequences of our actions. This means that we accept what happens because of our choices.

Sometimes we make a choice that we know God does not want us to make. We need to fix the harm our bad choices have done.

ACTIVITY Read this story. Write or draw one consequence of Sarah's choice.

### Sarah's Choice

Sarah's little sister Katie is sick. Sarah asks her parents, "May I read Katie a story?"

## The Gift of Our Conscience

God gives us a gift that helps us to make wise choices. This gift is our **conscience.** Our conscience tells us whether a choice we are about to make or a choice we have made is a wise choice.

We need to form our conscience. We need to learn what God wants us to do. We pray to the Holy Spirit. We read and listen to the Bible. We learn what the Church teaches. We ask our parents and other grown-ups to help us.

 *Read each statement and think about your day. Circle the happy and sad faces to help you to review the choices you made.*

# Thinking about Our Choices

1. I prayed to God to ask for help.  ☺ ☹

2. I showed my love to family members.  ☺ ☹

3. I showed my love to my friends.  ☺ ☹

4. I showed my love to other people.  ☺ ☹

# Our Church Makes a Difference

## Morning and Night Prayers

We can pray in the morning and at night. In the morning we ask God to help us to make wise choices.

We pray at night to help us to think about the day. We examine our conscience. We talk to God about the choices we have made. God helps us to make better and better choices.

We pray at the beginning and end of each day. This helps us to make choices to live as Jesus taught us to live. It helps us to thank and praise God all day long.

 *When do you pray each day? How does praying each day help people to make wise choices?*

### Our Catholic Faith

**Examination of Conscience**

We examine our conscience to know if the choices we made were wise choices. This helps us to live holy lives. We always examine our conscience to prepare for the celebration of the sacrament of Reconciliation.

# What Difference Does Faith Make in My Life?

Your conscience helps you to know right from wrong. It helps you to make choices to live as Jesus taught.

*Circle the pictures that show children making a good choice to live as Jesus taught. Write an X on the pictures that show a bad choice.*

## Making Choices

### My Faith Choice

I can choose to make choices to live as Jesus taught. This week I will

_____

_____.

### Prayer of Saint Francis

*Saint Francis of Assisi prayed about making wise choices. He prayed that God would help him to be a peacemaker. Peace happens when we live as God wants us to live.*

**All:** Lord, make us instruments of your peace.

**Group 1:** Where there is hatred,
**Group 2:** let us bring love.

**Group 1:** Where there is injury,
**Group 2:** let us bring forgiveness.

**All:** Lord, make us instruments of your peace.

## We Remember

*Unscramble the letters to make a word you learned in this chapter. Make up a sentence using the word. Share your sentence with others.*

SCICONENCE

C _ _ _ S C _ _ _ N _ _

**To Help You Remember**

1. We are happy when we make choices that follow God's will.

2. Wise choices show we are following our conscience.

3. All of our choices have consequences.

# 22 With My Family

## This Week . . .

In chapter 22, "We Make Choices," your child learned that we are responsible for the choices we make. God has given us the gift of a conscience to help us discern right from wrong. Every person has the responsibility to form a good conscience. Parents and others who have children under their care have the responsibility to help their children develop a well-formed and correct conscience. This will help the children live according to God's will and find happiness both here on earth and forever in heaven.

**For more** on the teachings of the Catholic Church on true happiness, responsibility, and conscience, see *Catechism of the Catholic Church* paragraph numbers 1716–1724, 1730–1738, and 1776–1794.

## Sharing God's Word

Read together Sirach 15:14–15 or read the adaptation of these verses on page 191. Emphasize that God created us with a free will and the ability to make our own choices.

## Praying

In this chapter your child prayed part of the peace prayer of Saint Francis of Assisi. Read and pray together the prayer on page 195.

## Making a Difference

Choose one of the following activities to do as a family or design a similar activity of your own.

- Watch a TV show together. Point out when characters on the show make wise choices and when they make bad choices. If someone makes a bad choice, make suggestions for a wise choice.

- Talk about how your family can help and support one another to make wise decisions and choices.

- Celebrate wise choices. At dinnertime this week share with one another the wise choices family members made during the day and talk about their consequences. Share how the good consequences of your choices help to build a world of peace and fairness.

For more ideas on ways your family can live your faith, visit the "Faith First for Families" page at **www.FaithFirst.com**. Click on "Saints." Talk about the consequences of the wise choices the saint made.

# We Share in God's Life

## We Pray

I trust God, who
    always cares
    for me.
        Based on Psalm 57:3

Lord God, we
bless you and
thank you. You
have called us
to share in
your life. Amen.

What is a favorite
gift you have
received?

A gift is a sign of
love. God gives us
the gift of sharing
in his life.

What does it mean
to share in the gift
of God's life?

# God Shares His Life with Us

## Faith Focus

What does the gift of grace help us to do?

## Faith Words

**sanctifying grace**
Sanctifying grace is the gift of God sharing his life with us.

## God Shares His Life with Us

God has given us the gift of **sanctifying grace.** The word *sanctifying* means "something that makes us holy." We first receive this gift at Baptism.

The gift of sanctifying grace makes us children of God. God shares his life with us. As God's children, filled with grace, we are holy. The Bible tells us,

Through your faith in Jesus, you are all children of God.

Based on Galatians 3:26

God also helps us to live as his children. The Holy Spirit always gives us the grace to make wise choices. This helps us to live as children of God.

**ACTIVITY** *Color the Xs one color. Color the Os different colors. Thank God for the wonderful gift of grace.*

## Choosing to Live a Holy Life

It is not always easy to choose to live a holy life. Sometimes we choose to sin. All sins hurt our relationship with God and other people. Some sins are very serious. These sins are mortal sins. When we commit a mortal sin, we lose the gift of sanctifying grace.

We need to confess mortal sins in the sacrament of Reconciliation. When we are sorry for our sins and confess them in Reconciliation, God forgives our sins. We receive the gift of sanctifying grace again.

Other sins are not as serious as mortal sins. These sins are venial sins. It is good to confess these sins too. In Reconciliation we receive God's grace to live a holy life.

 *What are some of the ways we can show we are truly sorry for our sins?*

Receiving absolution in sacrament of Reconciliation

## Jesus Teaches About Forgiveness

Jesus reminded us over and over again that God is always ready to forgive our sins. Jesus also taught us another important thing about forgiveness. We need to forgive other people. He said,

"Forgive and you will be forgiven."          Luke 6:37

The Holy Spirit always gives us the help to forgive others. Forgiving others is not always easy. When we forgive others, we are living the Great Commandment.

ACTIVITY *In one frame draw yourself forgiving someone. In the other frame draw someone forgiving you.*

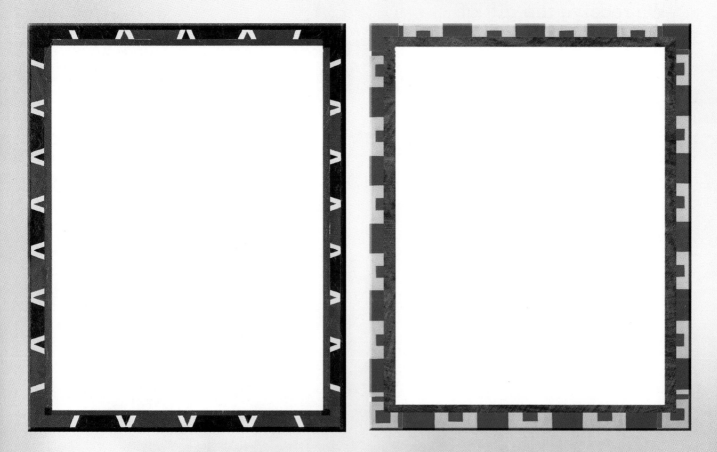

200

## Saint Catherine of Siena

Catherine of Siena lived at a time when the people in the Church were having disagreements. Some of these disagreements led to fighting.

Catherine helped people in the Church to see the harm their fighting was causing. She brought people together. They began to forgive one another and to solve their problems without fighting.

The Church celebrates the feast day of Saint Catherine of Siena on April 29. We ask the Holy Spirit to help us to forgive those who hurt us. We ask the Holy Spirit to help us to live as peacemakers.

 **QUESTION** *What are some of the ways you see people showing forgiveness to others?*

### Our Catholic Faith

**Religious Medals**

Catholics sometimes wear a cross or a religious medal of Mary or of a saint. This helps us to remember to live as children of God. It also helps us to remember to pray to Mary and the other saints to help us live as Jesus taught.

# What Difference Does Faith Make in My Life?

God shares the gift of his life with us. The Holy Spirit helps us to live as children of God. One way you can live as a child of God is to be a peacemaker.

*Work with your teacher or parent. Create a message for the Internet that tells how people your age can live as peacemakers.*

## Teaching Peace

## My Faith Choice

This week I will show I am a peacemaker. I will

_____

_____.

## Hail Mary

*Learn the Hail Mary by heart. Pray it every day to show your love for Mary. Ask Mary to help you to live a holy life.*

**Group 1:** Hail Mary, full of grace, the Lord is with you!

**Group 2:** Blessed are you among women, and blessed is the fruit of your womb, Jesus.

**All:** Holy Mary, Mother of God, pray for us sinners, now and at the hour of our death. Amen.

## We Remember

*Write words on the path that show ways we can live holy lives.*

**To Help You Remember**

1. Grace is a gift from God.

2. Sanctifying grace is the gift of God's life that he shares with us.

3. Other graces help us to live holy lives.

## This Week . . .

In chapter 23, "We Share in God's Life," your child learned that God shares divine life with us. We receive the gift of sanctifying grace. By sharing his life with us, God calls us to live a holy life. Sin turns us away from God's love and deters us from living holy lives. When we sin, we need to be sorry and ask God for forgiveness. Asking for forgiveness and forgiving others are part of living a holy life.

**For more** on the teachings of the Catholic Church on grace and the call to holiness, see *Catechism of the Catholic Church* paragraph numbers 1846–1869 and 1996–2016.

## Sharing God's Word

Read together Matthew 6:14–15. Emphasize that God gives us the gift of his help, or grace, to live as children of God. God helps us forgive others as he forgives us.

## Praying

In this chapter your child prayed the Hail Mary. Read and pray together the Hail Mary on page 203.

## Making a Difference

Choose one of the following activities to do as a family or design a similar activity of your own.

- Name people who have showed you ways to be forgiving. Discuss that when we do not make wise choices and sin, we need to be sorry and ask God for forgiveness. As God forgives us, we need to forgive others too.

- Become more familiar with the Hail Mary. Use the Hail Mary for your family prayer this week.

- Create forgiveness place mats. Use the place mats at family meals as reminders to forgive others as you want to be forgiven by God and others.

For more ideas on ways your family can live your faith, visit the "Faith First for Families" page at **www.FaithFirst.com**. As a family share some of the ideas on the "Gospel Reflections" page this week.

# Review Unit 3

Name _____

## A. The Best Word or Phrase

*Complete the sentences. Color the circle next to the best choice for each sentence.*

1. The Great ___ helps us to love God and to love our neighbor as ourselves.

   ○ Commandment      ○ Covenant      ○ Proverb

2. God gave us the Ten ___ to help us to live as children of God.

   ○ Covenants   ○ Commandments   ○ Works of Mercy

3. Our conscience tells us whether a choice we are going to make is a ___ one.

   ○ wise      ○ bad      ○ wise or bad

4. God's gift of sanctifying ___ makes us holy and children of God.

   ○ help      ○ love      ○ grace

5. A very serious sin is called a ___ sin.

   ○ mortal      ○ venial      ○ sanctifying

205

## B. The Ten Commandments

*Put a **G** in front of each sentence that tells us about loving God. Put an **O** in front of each sentence that tells about loving ourselves and other people.*

_____ 1. Keep one day each week for God.

_____ 2. Be honest and truthful.

_____ 3. Worship only God.

_____ 4. Honor and obey your parents.

_____ 5. Take care of and respect life.

## C. What I Have Learned

1. *Name two things you learned in this unit. Tell a partner.*

_____

_____

2. *Look at the words listed on page 156. Circle the ones that you know now.*

## D. From a Scripture Story

*The Book of Proverbs has sayings that help people to make wise choices. One proverb says, "Ask God's help before you do something" (based on Proverbs 16:3). Write or draw about a time when you will use this proverb.*

What are some ways that Catholics pray?

207

# Getting Ready

## What I Have Learned

*What is something you already know about prayer?*

Ways to pray

_____

_____

Places to pray

_____

_____

Praying the Our Father

_____

_____

## Words to Know

*Put an X next to the faith words you know. Put a ? next to words you need to know more about.*

### Faith Words

_____ prayer

_____ Lord's Prayer

_____ kingdom of God

_____ trust

## A Question I Have

*What question would you like to ask about the Our Father?*

_____

_____

_____

## A Scripture Story

Jesus teaching the Our Father

*Why did Jesus teach the Apostles the Our Father?*

# We Talk
# with God

## We Pray

All day long,
  praise the name
  of the LORD.
    Based on Psalm 113:3

**Lord our God,
listen to our
prayer.    Amen.**

*What do you like
to do with your
friends?*

Friends like to
spend time with
one another. God
wants us to spend
time with him.

*When are some
times that you talk
to God?*

# We Pray to God

## Talking to God

Jesus taught us to pray. **Prayer** is raising our hearts and minds to God. It is talking and listening to God. We share our thoughts and feelings with God when we pray.

In our prayers we tell God we love him. We ask God for his blessings and help. We ask for forgiveness. We thank and praise God for all he has done for us.

Sometimes we talk to God in quiet, soft voices. Sometimes we just think in our minds. Sometimes we sign our prayers. At other times we sing hymns or songs. Sometimes we pray using special actions or dance.

**QUESTION** *What is your favorite way to pray?*

210

## Listening to God

Prayer is not just about talking to God. It is also listening to God. God speaks to us in the Bible and sometimes through other people. God also speaks to us quietly in our own hearts and minds.

We do not need a special time or place to pray. We can pray anytime and anywhere. We can pray alone or with other people. God is always there ready to listen.

 *Draw your favorite place where you like to pray.*

### Faith-Filled People

**Maria von Trapp**

Maria's family lived at a time when people were suffering because of their religion. By singing with her children Maria taught them to trust in God's love. Maria's story has been shared with the world in the movie *The Sound of Music.*

### Praying in a Special Place

## Praying During the Day

Praying at special times helps us to make prayer an important part of each day. At the beginning of the day, we ask God to bless us and our family. We ask God to help us to make good choices all day.

Many times during the day, we take time to think about God. At the end of the day, we thank God for helping us to be kind. We tell God we are sorry for any wrong we may have done. We ask God to help us to make up with anyone we may have hurt.

**ACTIVITY**

Write a one-sentence prayer to pray in the morning when you wake up.

_____

_____

_____

_____

# Our Church Makes a Difference

## Blessed Kateri Tekakwitha

Kateri Tekakwitha was a Native American. She was a member of the Turtle Clan of the Iroquois.

Kateri loved to go into the woods and be alone with God. Her favorite place to pray was in the tall trees amid the quiet sounds. "There," she said, "God speaks to my heart."

The Church honors Kateri Tekakwitha as "Blessed." The Church names a person "Blessed" before it names a person a saint.

**QUESTION?** *Who do you know who both prays and does kind things for other people? What does that person do?*

### Our Catholic Faith

**Family Prayer**

We first learn to pray in our families. Families often pray at mealtimes. Another favorite time for families to pray is at the end of the day before bedtime.

# What Difference Does Faith Make in My Life?

The Holy Spirit asks you to make prayer an important part of your life. The Holy Spirit invites you to pray often during the day.

## Talking with God

*On the clock, circle three times during the day when you might pray. On the lines below write the times you circled and prayers you can say.*

8 : 0 0     Thank you, God, for a new day!

___ : ___ ___     _____

___ : ___ ___     _____

___ : ___ ___     _____

### My Faith Choice

*ff* This week I will try my best to pray several times each day. I will

_____

_____.

## Spending Time with God

*Here are a few steps you can use to pray anytime and anywhere. Use them each day. Practice them now.*

**1.** Be very quiet.

**2.** Believe that God is present with you.

**3.** Think about what you want to share with God. Share it.

**4.** Think about what God might be saying to you. Listen.

**5.** Thank God for being with you.

## We Remember

*Draw a* ✔ *next to each statement you agree with. Draw an* ✗ *next to each statement you do not agree with. Give a reason for each* ✔ *and each* ✗*.*

___ **1.** We can tell God about anything.

___ **2.** We must wait our turn before God is ready to listen.

___ **3.** We can pray anytime.

___ **4.** God always listens to our prayers.

**To Help You Remember**

1. When we pray, we talk and listen to God.

2. When we pray, we show that we trust God.

3. When we pray, we make God part of our day.

## This Week . . .

In chapter 24, "We Talk with God," your child learned the importance of prayer in the life of a follower of Jesus. Jesus taught us the importance of prayer by his example. Our Christian family is the first place we learn to pray. We can pray anywhere and anytime. God is always present, listening and responding to our prayer.

**For more** on the teachings of the Catholic Church on the prayer of Jesus and the many expressions of Christian prayer, see *Catechism of the Catholic Church* paragraph numbers 2559–2616 and 2697–2719.

## Sharing God's Word

Read together 1 Thessalonians 5:17. Emphasize that we are to pray often during the day.

## Praying

In this chapter your child learned some steps that can be used for prayer anywhere and anytime. Read these steps on page 215 together. Take the time this week to follow the steps to pray alone and as a family.

## Making a Difference

Choose one of the following activities to do as a family or design a similar activity of your own.

- We can pray anywhere and anytime. Ask each family member to share where and when they pray.

- We learn to pray first in our families. Talk about your family prayer times. Discuss how and when you pray as a family. Decide on times you will pray as a family this week.

- Write a family prayer thanking God for each family member. Pray this prayer at dinnertime this week.

For more ideas on ways your family can live your faith, visit the "Faith First for Families" page at **www.FaithFirst.com**. Click on "Family Prayer" to find a special prayer to pray this week.

# Jesus Teaches Us to Pray

## A Scripture Story

## We Pray

Come, let us sing
to God.
Based on Psalm 95:1

**Lord Jesus,
teach us to pray.
Amen.**

*Who first taught
you to pray?*

We first learn to
pray at home.
People in our
Church also teach
us to pray. Jesus
taught his disciples
to pray.

*What did Jesus
teach about prayer?*

Jesus teaching the
people about the
kingdom of God

217

# Bible Background

## Faith Focus

Why do we pray to God the Father?

## Faith Words

**Lord's Prayer**
The Lord's Prayer is another name for the Our Father.

## Jesus Prayed

Jesus lived in Galilee. Galilee is a large area of land with mountains, lakes, and fields.

Jesus prayed in many places in Galilee. He prayed alone in quiet places. He prayed in the mountains and in the fields. He prayed with other people.

When he prayed, Jesus asked his Father what he wanted him to do. He told his Father that he would do whatever the Father asked him. Jesus knew and trusted that his Father was always listening.

*Find and circle four places you can pray. On the line write your favorite place to pray. Share with a partner why it is your favorite place to pray.*

### God Is Always with Us

```
D B L H O M E T P K
L Q R P A R K G T B
P L A Y G R O U N D
N C H U R C H Q V W
```

_____

# Reading the Word of God

## Jesus Teaches the Disciples to Pray

One day Jesus went up a mountain to pray. His disciples went with him. They wanted Jesus to teach them to pray. This is what Jesus taught them.

"This is how you are to pray.
Our Father in heaven,
    hallowed be your name,
    your kingdom come,
    your will be done,
      on earth as in heaven.
Give us today our daily bread;
and forgive us our debts,
as we forgive our debtors;
and lead us not into temptation,
    but deliver us from evil."
Based on Matthew 6:9–13

Jesus taught the disciples to pray to God the Father. He taught them to love and trust his Father as he did.

 *When do you pray the Our Father?*

219

## The Lord's Prayer

We also call the Our Father the **Lord's Prayer.** We call it the Lord's Prayer because it is the prayer that Jesus our Lord taught the disciples. The Our Father is the prayer of the whole Church. Catholics all over the world pray the Our Father every day.

*Draw yourself in the picture. Imagine you are with children from all over the world. Silently pray the Our Father with them.*

# Our Church Makes a Difference

## A Life of Prayer

Some people in the Church pray every day, all day long. Convent, abbey, and monastery are three names we give to the places they live.

These people of prayer remind us that God is the Father of all people. They pray for the Church and for the whole world.

 **QUESTION** *What problem in the world would you like to pray for?*

Chapel at Christ of the Desert Monastery

Trappist Monks at Mepkin Abbey

Sisters of the Precious Blood at prayer in convent

221

# What Difference Does Faith Make in My Life?

Children all the world over pray each day. Join with all Christian children and pray the Our Father. Show you love and trust in God the Father.

*Finish this prayer to God our Father. Use the words in the word box and sign you name.*

## God Our Father

Dear God,

You are our loving _____.

Help me to live as your _____.

Help me to _____ people,

as you forgive me.

Thank you.

_____

**Word box:** forgive · Father · child

## My Faith Choice

This week I will pray the Our Father every day. I will pray it

❑ in the morning.    ❑ at bedtime.

❑ at mealtimes.    ❑ _____.
                                    *another time*

## We Pray

### Psalm 23

*Psalms are prayer songs. Psalm 23 tells us that God always cares for his people. Close your eyes and listen as the leader reads the words. Talk to God in your own words.*

**Leader:** The Lord is my shepherd;
I shall not want.
He guides me in right paths
for his name's sake.

Based on Psalm 23:1, 3

**All:** *Talk silently to God in your own words.*

## We Remember

*Fill in the spaces. Use the words in the word bank.*

**Father    heaven    kingdom**

Our _____ who art in

_____, hallowed be thy name;

thy _____ come.

**To Help You Remember**

1. Jesus often prayed to his Father.

2. Jesus taught his disciples to pray the Our Father.

3. The Church prays the Our Father every day.

## This Week . . .

In chapter 25, "Jesus Teaches Us to Pray: A Scripture Story," your child listened to the Scripture story of Jesus teaching the disciples to pray. The disciples learned to pray from watching Jesus pray. When they asked him to teach them to pray, Jesus taught the disciples the Our Father. The Our Father is also called the Lord's Prayer. It is the prayer of the whole Church, of all Christians. The Church prays the Our Father every day. We pray it as a Church community at every Mass.

**For more** on the teachings of the Catholic Church on Jesus as our model and teacher for prayer, see *Catechism of the Catholic Church* paragraph numbers 2598–2615, 2746–2751, and 2759.

## Sharing God's Word

Read together the Bible story in Matthew 6:9–13 about Jesus teaching the disciples how to pray or read the adaptation of the story on page 219. Emphasize that the Church prays the Our Father every day.

## Praying

In this chapter your child prayed a prayer based on Psalm 23:1–3. Read and pray the prayer on page 223.

## Making a Difference

Choose one of the following activities to do as a family or design a similar activity of your own.

- Make a puzzle to help you become more familiar with the Our Father. Write the Our Father on a piece of paper. Cut the paper into smaller puzzle pieces. Next assemble the puzzle to help your child learn the Our Father.

- We can pray anytime and anywhere. Talk about your family prayer. Use these and similar questions: What do we pray for? Who do we pray for? What do we tell God about?

- When you take part in Mass this week and pray the Our Father, remember that Catholics all over the world pray the Our Father with you.

For more ideas on ways your family can live your faith, visit the "Faith First for Families" page at **www.FaithFirst.com**. This week take time to read an article from "Just for Parents."

# The Our Father

## We Pray

God's love for us
lasts forever.
*Based on Psalm 136:1*

**God our Father,
we praise you
with the whole
Church, all the
world over.
Amen.**

*What are new
things you have
learned this year?*

This year we have
learned what it
means to be a child
of God. Jesus taught
his disciples the
Our Father.

*What is one thing
you know about the
Our Father?*

# We Pray the Our Father

## Faith Focus

Why do we pray the Our Father?

## Faith Words

**kingdom of God**
The kingdom of God is also called the kingdom of heaven.

## The Our Father

The Our Father helps us to pray and understand how to live as God's children.

**Our Father, Who Art in Heaven:** God is the Father of all people. God creates us in his image and likeness. God shares his life and love with us now and forever.

**Hallowed Be Thy Name:** The word *hallowed* means "very holy." We love God above all else. We adore and worship God. We honor and respect the name of God in all we say and do.

**Thy Kingdom Come:** Jesus announced the coming of the **kingdom of God.** The kingdom of God is also called the kingdom of heaven. When we love God above all else, we live as Jesus taught. We prepare for the coming of the kingdom of God.

 *What are the things you do and say that show your love for God the Father?*

**Thy Will Be Done on Earth as It Is in Heaven:** The Holy Spirit helps us to continue the work of Jesus. We share God's love with our family, friends, and everyone we meet.

### Benedict

Saint Benedict wrote a set of rules. These rules helped people to make praying the center of each day. Many people used the Rule of Saint Benedict to guide their lives. People who follow the Rule of Saint Benedict are called Benedictines. The Church celebrates the feast day of Saint Benedict on July 11.

**Give Us This Day Our Daily Bread:** We always trust God. God knows what we need. We ask God to help us to live as his children. We pray for all people to receive God's blessings.

*Draw lines to connect each part of the Our Father to its meaning.*

| | |
|---|---|
| Our Father | God's name is said with love. |
| In heaven | God's love for us is now and forever. |
| Hallowed be thy name | God is the Father of all. |
| Thy kingdom come | The kingdom of God is called heaven. |
| Thy will be done | God gives us what we need. |
| Give us this day our daily bread | We continue the work of Jesus. |

**And Forgive Us Our Trespasses as We Forgive Those Who Trespass Against Us:** Jesus taught us to be forgiving persons. Asking for forgiveness and forgiving others help us to live as children of God and followers of Jesus.

**And Lead Us Not into Temptation, But Deliver Us from Evil:** We ask God to help us to say no to temptation. Temptation is everything that can lead us away from God's love and from living as children of God. The Holy Spirit helps us to make wise choices. The Holy Spirit helps us to say no to temptation and all that is evil.

**Amen:** We end our prayer by saying, "Amen." *Amen* means, "Yes, it is true. We believe!"

*Draw lines to connect each part of the Our Father to its meaning.*

| And forgive us our trespasses as we forgive those who trespass against us | We ask God to protect us. |
| Lead us not into temptation | We believe! |
| But deliver us from evil | We ask God to help us to choose good. |
| Amen | God forgives us as we forgive others. |

# Our Church Makes a Difference

## The Family of God

God calls everyone who is baptized to live as a follower of Jesus. God calls many men and women to live a married life. God also calls some people to live a single life.

God calls some men to serve the whole Church as bishops, priests, and deacons. He calls other men to live in a religious community as priests, deacons, or brothers. He calls some women to live in a religious community as sisters.

Whatever way God calls us to live, we are all members of God's family. We work together to continue the work of Jesus. We prepare for the kingdom of God.

## Our Catholic Faith

### Vocation

The word *vocation* means "what we are called to do." Every Christian has the vocation to live as a follower of Jesus. God calls us to do this in different ways in the Church.

*QUESTION*

*What do you want to do when you grow up? How will it help you to live as a follower of Jesus?*

# What Difference Does Faith Make in My Life?

The Holy Spirit is helping you to live the Our Father now. He is helping you to live as a member of the family of God's people.

*Put a ✔ next to one way that you will try to live the words of the Our Father this summer. Make a plan to put your choice into action.*

## Living as Jesus Taught

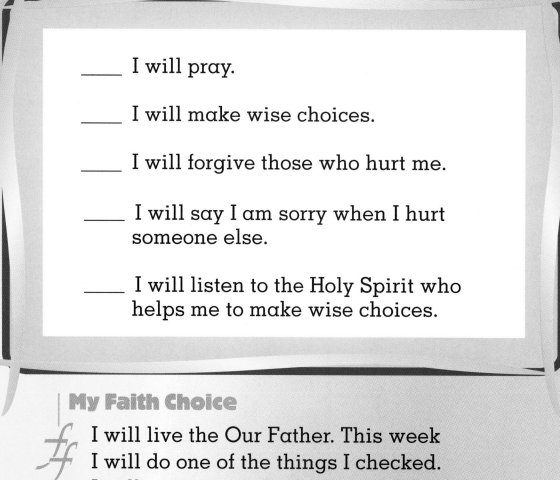

_____ I will pray.

_____ I will make wise choices.

_____ I will forgive those who hurt me.

_____ I will say I am sorry when I hurt someone else.

_____ I will listen to the Holy Spirit who helps me to make wise choices.

### My Faith Choice

I will live the Our Father. This week I will do one of the things I checked. I will continue to do the things I checked all summer.

## Go Forth!

*Jesus taught that we must live our faith in God. Thank God for all you learned this year. Live your faith and make a difference.*

**Leader:** Lord, each day we will remember and act like children of God.

**All:** **Thanks be to God!**

**Leader:** Lord, we will love and serve you every day.

**All:** **Thanks be to God!**

**Leader:** Lord, we will treat others with kindness.

**All:** **Thanks be to God!**

## We Remember

*Use the clues to solve the puzzle.*

**DOWN**

1. ____ means "very holy."

2. When you ____, you lift up your heart to God.

**ACROSS**

3. God is our ____.

4. ____ is something that leads us away from God.

5. Living as God wants us to live helps us to prepare for the ____ of God.

| CLUES | |
|---|---|
| Temptation | pray |
| kingdom | Father |
| Hallowed | |

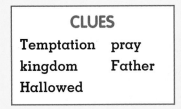

**To Help You Remember**

1. We pray the Our Father to show our love and adoration of God.

2. The Our Father helps us to live as children of God.

3. The Our Father helps us to prepare for the kingdom of God.

## This Week . . .

In chapter 26, "The Our Father," your child learned the meaning of the parts, or petitions, of the Our Father. The Our Father is not only a prayer. It is also a school of prayer. Praying the Our Father teaches us how we are to pray. When we pray the Our Father, we understand what it means to live as children of God and to prepare for the coming of the kingdom of God.

**For more** on the teachings of the Catholic Church on the parts of the Our Father, see *Catechism of the Catholic Church* paragraph numbers 2777–2856.

## Sharing God's Word

Read together Matthew 6:9–13. Emphasize that the Our Father is not only a prayer. It is a "summary of the whole Gospel." Praying the Our Father teaches us how to pray and how to live as children of God.

## Praying

In this chapter your child prayed a prayer of thanksgiving. Read and pray together the prayer on page 231.

## Making a Difference

Choose one of the following activities to do as a family or design a similar activity of your own.

• Make an Our Father booklet. As you read each part of the Our Father, write the words of that part in your booklet. Write or draw how you can live each part of the Our Father.

• Talk about some of the ways your family lives the Our Father. Pray to the Holy Spirit. Ask the Holy Spirit to help your family live the Our Father.

• Ask each family member to name one thing they learned about the Our Father from this chapter. Afterward, pray the Our Father together.

For more ideas on ways your family can live your faith, visit the "Faith First for Families" page at **www.FaithFirst.com**. "Gospel Reflections" will continue to change each week over the summer. Don't forget to check it out.

## A. The Best Word or Phrase

*Complete the sentences. Color the circle next to the best choice for each sentence.*

1. ___ is raising our hearts and minds to God.

   ○ Standing      ○ Praying      ○ Kneeling

2. Jesus taught his disciples the ___.

   ○ Hail Mary      ○ Glory Prayer      ○ Our Father

3. The kingdom of ___ is all people living as God wants them to live.

   ○ saints      ○ God      ○ earth

4. We can pray ___.

   ○ anytime      ○ on Sundays      ○ at bedtime

5. We can pray ___.

   ○ anywhere      ○ at home      ○ in church

## B. Making Sentences

*Color the box to mark the sentences that are true.*

☐ Jesus taught us to pray to God the Father.

☐ God speaks to us quietly in our minds and hearts.

☐ We can always thank God for his blessings.

☐ We can only pray in Church.

## C. What I Have Learned

1. *Name two things you learned in this unit. Tell a partner.*

_____

_____

2. *Look at the words listed on page 208. Circle the ones that you know now.*

## D. From a Scripture Story

*Draw lines to connect the parts of the Our Father to their meanings.*

**Parts**

1. Our Father
2. Hallowed be thy name
3. Give us this day our daily bread
4. Forgive us our trespasses as we forgive those who trespass against us
5. Deliver us from evil

**Meanings**

a. God gives us what we need.

b. God forgives us as we forgive others.

c. God is the Father of all.

d. We ask God to protect us.

e. God's name is said with love.

How does the Church celebrate its faith all year long?

235

# The Liturgical Year

The Church's year of prayer and worship is called the liturgical year. These are the seasons of the Church's year.

## Advent

We prepare for Christmas. The color for Advent is purple.

## Christmas

We praise and thank God for sending us Jesus, the Savior of the world. The color for Christmas is white.

## Lent

We make sacrifices to help us to remember our love for God and others. We prepare for Easter. The color for Lent is purple.

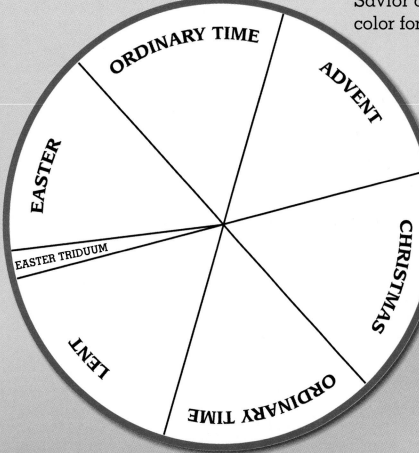

## Easter Triduum

Triduum is the three days during Holy Week when we remember Jesus' death and Resurrection. We welcome new members into the Church.

## Easter

For fifty days we celebrate and remember and share in Jesus' Resurrection. The color for Easter is white.

## Ordinary Time

The rest of the Church's year is called Ordinary Time. We learn to live as followers of Jesus. The color for Ordinary Time is green.

*ACTIVITY* Color each of the seasons of the Church on the chart. What is your favorite season? Tell one thing you can do to celebrate it.

# Ordinary Time

## The Word of the Lord

These are the Gospel readings for the Third Sunday in Ordinary Time. Ask your family to read this year's Gospel reading with you. Talk about the reading with your family.

Year A
  Matthew 4:12–23 or
  Matthew 4:12–17

Year B
  Mark 1:14–20

Year C
  Luke 1:1–4, 4:14–21

## What You See

When we see the color green, we think of plants and other living things. The color green reminds us of the life we are living as Christians.

## The Celebrations of Our Church

Birthday parties are fun. So are Christmas parties and parties with our teammates. We seem to have something to celebrate all throughout the year.

Our Church celebrates our faith all year long too. We celebrate during the seasons of Advent and Christmas, Lent and Easter, and Ordinary Time.

Each week at Mass we listen to a different story from the Gospel. We hear Jesus teaching his disciples. Closing our eyes, we can imagine we are with Jesus. We think about what Jesus is saying and doing. We decide how we can live as a follower of Jesus.

# Living Our Faith

*Think about your favorite stories about Jesus. Draw one of those stories in this box. Share how this story helps you to live as a follower of Jesus.*

# The First Week of Advent

## Faith Focus

How does celebrating Advent help us to welcome God into our lives?

## The Word of the Lord

These are the Gospel readings for the First Sunday of Advent. Ask your family to read this year's Gospel reading with you. Talk about the reading with them.

Year A
  Matthew 24:37–44

Year B
  Mark 13:33–37

Year C
  Luke 21:25–28, 34–36

## What You See

The Advent wreath is made of evergreens. There are three purple candles and one pink candle. The candles stand for the four weeks of Advent.

## Getting Ready

Every year you get excited about your birthday coming. Your family gets ready to celebrate. During Advent we get ready to celebrate the birth of Jesus. We also celebrate that Jesus is always with us. We celebrate that he will come in glory at the end of the world.

Advent has four Sundays. On these Sundays we gather in our parish church. Together we get our hearts ready to welcome Jesus.

During Advent we remember that Jesus asks us to do good things. We pray. We try to be extra kind. We help people who need our help.

# We Welcome Jesus

*Think about ways you can get ready to welcome Jesus. Write something you can do each day this week.*

| | |
|---|---|
| **Sunday** | Use the Advent wreath at dinnertime. |
| **Monday** | call my grandmother |
| **Tuesday** | Help my mom with the dishes. |
| **Wednesday** | call my father |
| **Thursday** | clean my room without my mom asking me |
| **Friday** | I'll do my homwork on my own |
| **Saturday** | Help my mom clean the house. |

# The Third Week of Advent

## Faith Focus

How do we show our hope in God during Advent?

## The Word of the Lord

These are the Gospel readings for the Third Sunday of Advent. Ask your family to read this year's Gospel reading with you. Talk about the reading with them.

Year A
   Matthew 11:2–11

Year B
   John 1:6–8, 19–28

Year C
   Luke 3:10–18

## Hope in God

Sometimes we need people we trust to help us. The Bible tells us that God is our helper. We can always trust God.

During Advent we praise God too. We remember the story of God's promises to us. We believe that God is always near. We are filled with hope that God will come again in glory at the end of the world. We will celebrate that faith and hope with great joy during Advent.

# People of Joy

 In each green leaf write one way someone has brought you joy. In each yellow leaf write one way you can bring joy to someone. Make a plan and put your choice into action this Advent.

# The Fourth Week of Advent

## Faith Focus

Why was Jesus born in Bethlehem?

## The Word of the Lord

These are the Gospel readings for the Fourth Sunday of Advent. Ask your family to read this year's Gospel reading with you. Talk about the reading with them.

Year A
  Matthew 1:18–24

Year B
  Luke 1:26–33

Year C
  Luke 1:39–45

## Little Bethlehem

People live in small towns all over the world. Very often people who have become famous were born in these small towns. Long ago a man named David lived in the small town of Bethlehem. He became king of God's people.

Years later another leader wanted to know how many people lived in his land. So everyone had to go to their family's hometown to be counted. Joseph and Mary went to Bethlehem because Joseph belonged to David's family.

The prophet Micah said that the Savior who God promised to send his people would come from Bethlehem. Just as Micah said, Jesus was born in Bethlehem.

# The Legend of the Christmas Donkey

 *Read this story as a group. Think about the story. Decide ways you can be kind to others.*

**All:** Mary and Joseph had to go to Bethlehem. They walked a long way.

**Reader 1:** Mary was going to have a baby. She was very tired. Joseph saw a donkey eating grass nearby. He lifted Mary up onto the donkey's back.

**All:** The donkey was a peaceful animal. He felt honored to help Mary. He proudly carried Mary uphill and downhill.

**Reader 2:** When they got to the stable, Mary slipped off the donkey's back. She thanked him for his service.

**All:** From that day to this day, some donkeys bear the trace of a cross on their back. People say this is a sign that God rewards the smallest acts of kindness.

This week I will try to do one small act of kindness each day. One thing I will do is

_____

_____ .

# The First Week of Christmas

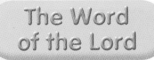

## Faith Focus

Why did the angels visit the shepherds?

## The Word of the Lord

This is the Gospel reading for Mass on Christmas Day. Ask your family to read it with you. Talk about the reading with them.

Year A, B, and C
    Luke 2:1–14

## What You See

The Christmas tree is made up of evergreens. It reminds us that God always loves us.

## The Good News of Jesus' Birth

Sometimes people tell us good news. Angels told good news to shepherds. They told the shepherds the good news of the birth of Jesus.

The angels praised God for this good news. They sang,

"Glory to God in the highest and on earth peace to those on whom his favor rests."

Luke 2:14

At Mass we sing this great song of the angels. We call it the "Gloria." We use their words to sing, "Glory to God in the highest and peace to his people on earth."

# Give Glory to God

*Color in the letters of this prayer. Pray the prayer each day of the Christmas season when you wake up. Pray it again at bedtime.*

# The First Week of Lent

## Faith Focus

How does celebrating Lent help us to get ready for Easter?

## The Word of the Lord

These are Gospel readings for the First Sunday of Lent. Ask your family to read this year's Gospel reading with you. Talk about the reading with them.

Year A
   Matthew 4:1–11

Year B
   Mark 1:12–15

Year C
   Luke 4:1–13

## What You See

During Lent the Church uses the color purple or violet. The colors purple and violet remind us of sorrow and penance.

## Keeping Lent

Sometimes a special day seems far away. But we can do many things to get ready for that day.

Lent is forty days long. It begins on Ash Wednesday. We turn to God and pray each day. We make sacrifices, or give up some things. This helps us to show our love for God and others.

Lent is the special time of the year the Church prepares new members for Baptism. It is the time members of the Church prepare to renew the promises we made at Baptism.

We do all these things during Lent to help us to prepare for Easter. Easter is a special day for all Christians. It is the day of Jesus' Resurrection.

# Prepare for Easter

 Pick a partner. Take turns answering each question. Decide how to keep Lent and prepare for Easter. On the lines write your answers to each question.

## LENT

**When does Lent begin?**

ash Wednesday

**How long is Lent?**

forty days

**What does the word *sacrifice* mean?**

Give up something

**What can you give up during Lent?**

give up my skateboard

**How can you help others during Lent?**

clean my room.

**What prayer could you say during Lent?**

Glory to God

## EASTER

# The Second Week of Lent

## Faith Focus

How can people know we are followers of Jesus?

## The Word of the Lord

These are the Gospel readings for the Second Sunday of Lent. Ask your family to read this year's Gospel reading with you. Talk about the reading with them.

Year A
Matthew 17:1–9

Year B
Mark 9:2–10

Year C
Luke 9:28–36

## The Vine and the Branches

Jesus once compared himself and his followers to a grape vine and its branches. Where Jesus lived grapevines grew on hillsides. The vine and the branches make juicy, sweet grapes.

Jesus said he is like the vine. We are his branches. We share his life. Together with Jesus we share God's love with others. During Lent we grow strong like the grape branches. We do good deeds. People know that we are followers of Jesus.

At Baptism we become one with Jesus. We promise to believe and do what he taught us.

# A Prayer for Growing as a Disciple of Jesus

*At Baptism we were joined to Christ. We became disciples of Christ. Lent is a time to grow as disciples of Jesus. Pray this prayer together.*

**Leader:** Living God, plant your love deep within us.

**All:** **Bring us to new life.**

**Leader:** Living God, you sent your Son, Jesus, to be one with us.

**All:** **Bring us to new life.**

**Leader:** Living God, send the Holy Spirit. May our words and actions be like the words and actions of Jesus.

**All:** **Bring us to new life.**

**Leader:** Living God, may we share the good news of your love with others, as Jesus did.

**All:** **Amen! Bring us to new life.**

## Faith Focus

How can we remember Jesus' journey to the place where he died?

## The Word of the Lord

These are the Gospel readings for the Third Sunday of Lent. Ask your family to read this year's Gospel reading with you. Talk about the reading with them.

Year A
  John 4:5–42 or
  John 4:5–15, 19–26,
    39, 40–44

Year B
  John 2:13–25

Year C
  Luke 13:1–9

## The Stations of the Cross

Who do you know who has died? What do you remember about that person? What do you do that helps you to remember that person? As we prepare for Easter we remember that Jesus died for us.

Long ago people went to Jerusalem to remember that Jesus died. They walked the same roads as he did to the place where he died on the cross. Along the way they stopped and prayed. Each place they stopped is called a station. The whole journey is called the Stations, or Way, of the Cross.

During Lent some Christians still go to Jerusalem to pray the Way of the Cross. Many others pray the Stations of the Cross in their parish churches. Today most churches have fourteen Stations of the Cross. Some have a fifteenth station. This station shows that Jesus, who died, is risen.

# The Cross of Christ

*The cross is a sign of Jesus' love for us. Use the code to discover a prayer about the cross. Learn the prayer by heart and pray it each day during Lent.*

1 = A   2 = E   3 = I   4 = O   5 = U

J __ sus,
   2

thr __ __ gh   th __   cr __ ss
     4   5         2       4

y __ __   br __ __ ght   j __ y
  4   5      4   5         4

t __   th __   w __ rld.
  4       2      4

Th __ nk   y __ __.
    1         4   5

Am __ n.
     2

## Faith Focus

During Lent how can we make more room in our hearts for God?

## The Word of the Lord

These are the Gospel readings for the Fourth Sunday of Lent. Ask your family to read this year's Gospel reading with you. Talk about the reading with them.

Year A
   John 9:1–41 or
   John 9:1, 6–9, 13–17,
      34–38

Year B
   John 3:14–21

Year C
   Luke 15:1–3,
      11–32

## Making Room for God

No matter how much we have, we can always share what we have with someone else.

Once a young man asked Jesus how to live as God wanted him to live. Knowing the young man owned many good things, Jesus told him to share his things with others. This would help the man to make more room in his heart for God.

During Lent the Church helps us to make room in our hearts for God too. We can do this by sharing our time, our talents, and our treasure with others.

We can use our time to visit someone who is sick. We can use our talents to help others. We can share the things we treasure with those who have too little.

# Sharing with Others

Jesus told us to share the blessings God gives us with others. In the boxes draw or write ways you can share your time, talents, and treasures with people. This week try your best to do what you have drawn or written in each gift box.

## Faith Focus

How can we grow as people who forgive others as God forgives us?

## The Word of the Lord

These are the Gospel readings for the Fifth Sunday of Lent. Ask your family to read this year's Gospel reading with you. Talk about the reading with them.

Year A
John 11:1–45 or
John 11:3–7, 17, 20–27,
    33–45

Year B
John 12:20–33

Year C
John 8:1–11

## A Forgiving Heart

When people hurt us, we sometimes want to hurt them back. Jesus asks us to forgive those who hurt us.

In the Our Father we pray "forgive us our trespasses as we forgive those who trespass against us." Praying these words shows that we want to forgive others. We want to have a forgiving heart.

During Lent we remember that God forgives us over and over. We try to forgive others over and over too.

We also celebrate God's forgiveness in the sacrament of Reconciliation during Lent. We come together with people in our parish and ask God for forgiveness of our sins. We ask God to help us to forgive others.

# FORGIVE US OUR TRESPASSES

# Growing in Forgiveness

*Lent is a time of forgiveness. The Our Father teaches that God forgives us and that we are to forgive others. Listen and pray together.*

## God's Word

**Leader:** Let us listen to a reading from Matthew's Gospel.

**Reader:** Peter asked Jesus, "Lord, if my brother sins against me, how often must I forgive him? As many as seven times?"

**Children: Jesus answered, "I say to you, not seven times, but seventy-seven times."**

Matthew 18:21–22

## Reflection and Prayer

**Leader:** Let us think of those people we forgive . . .
Let us now pray the Our Father and ask God to forgive us as we forgive others.

**All: Our Father . . .**

## Blessing

**Leader:** May God who calls you to grow as forgiving children bless you.

**All: Amen.**

**Leader:** May God who forgives over and over smile on you.

**All: Amen.**

**Leader:** May God who loves gather you in his tender care.

**All: Amen.**

# Palm Sunday of the Lord's Passion

## Faith Focus

How do we begin our celebration of Holy Week?

## The Word of the Lord

These are the Gospel readings for Palm Sunday of the Lord's Passion. Ask your family to read this year's Gospel reading with you. Talk about the reading with them.

Year A
Matthew 26:14–27,66 or
Matthew 27:11–54

Year B
Mark 14:1–15:47 or
Mark 15:1–39

Year C
Luke 22:14–23:56 or
Luke 23:1–49

## What You See

We carry palm branches in procession. We hold them as we listen to the Gospel reading.

## Holy Week Begins

When friends come to visit, we welcome them. Once when Jesus came to visit Jerusalem, many people came out to welcome him. They spread cloaks and branches on the road to honor him. The Church remembers and celebrates that special time on Palm Sunday of the Lord's Passion. It is the first day of Holy Week. Holy Week is the week before Easter.

At Mass on Palm Sunday we honor Jesus. We hold palm branches and say, "Hosanna to the Son of David. Blessed is he who comes in the name of the Lord!" We welcome Jesus as the people welcomed him to Jerusalem.

# We Honor Jesus

People sometimes carry banners in procession. Sometimes we hang banners in our church. Banners in our church help us to remember the liturgical season or feast we are celebrating. Decorate this banner. Use palm branches in the border.

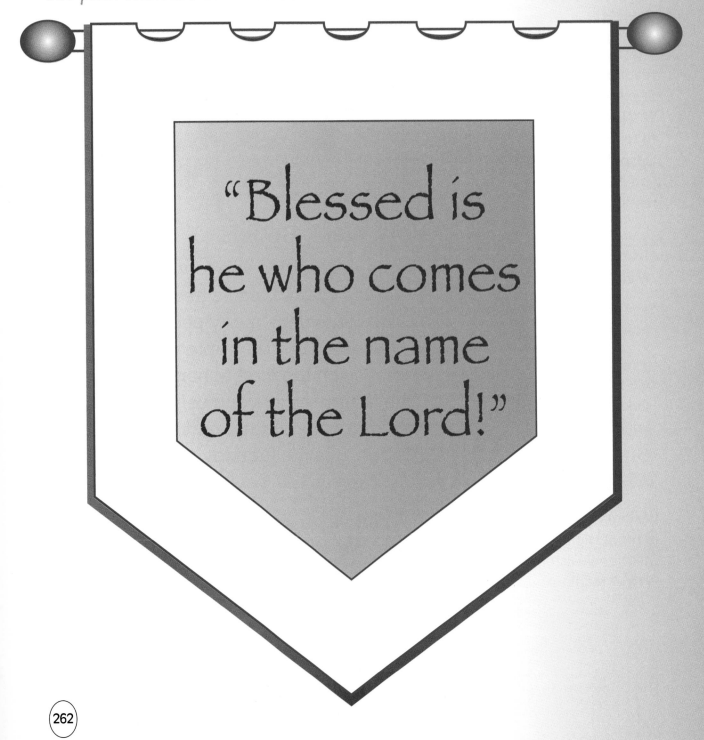

"Blessed is he who comes in the name of the Lord!"

# Triduum/Holy Thursday

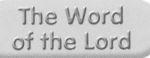

## Faith Focus

How does celebrating Holy Thursday help us to grow as followers of Jesus Christ?

## The Word of the Lord

These are the Scripture readings for the Mass of the Lord's Supper on Holy Thursday. Ask your family to read one of the readings with you. Talk about the reading with them.

First Reading
   Exodus 12:1–8, 11–14

Second Reading
   1 Corinthians 11:23–26

Gospel
   John 13:1–15

## What You See

The priest washes the feet of members of the parish. This reminds us that we are to help others as Jesus taught us.

## The Last Supper

Many things happen at a family meal. We prepare and cook food. We set the table. We clean up. When we do all these things, we are serving one another.

On Holy Thursday we remember how Jesus showed his love by serving his disciples. Before Jesus and his disciples ate the meal at the Last Supper, he washed their feet. After he finished, he told them to serve others as he served them.

On Holy Thursday we remember all Jesus did at the Last Supper. We especially remember that Jesus gave us the Eucharist.

# Prayer Service for Holy Thursday

*The hymn "Where Charity and Love are Found" is sung in many churches on Holy Thursday. The words of this hymn remind us that God is love. We are to love one another as Jesus loved us. Pray this prayer with your class.*

**Child 1:** The love of Christ gathers us.

**All:** **Where charity and love are found, there is God.**

**Child 2:** Let us be glad and rejoice in him.

**All:** **Where charity . . .**

**Child 3:** Let us love each other deep in our hearts.

**All:** **Where charity . . .**

**Child 4:** Let all people live in peace.

**All:** **Where charity . . .**

**Child 5:** Let Christ be in our midst.

**All:** **Where charity . . .**

**Child 6:** With all the blessed, may we enjoy the presence of Christ forever.

**All:** **Where charity . . .**

# Triduum/Good Friday

How does celebrating Good Friday help us to grow as followers of Christ?

## The Word of the Lord

These are the Scripture readings for Good Friday. Ask your family to read the readings with you. Talk about each reading with them.

First Reading
  Isaiah 52:13–53:12

Second Reading
  Hebrews 4:14–16,
    5:7–9

Gospel
  John 18:1–19:42

## The Crucifixion

Sometimes something happens to us that brings us suffering. We call this a cross. On Good Friday we remember that Jesus died on the cross. We listen to the story of his suffering and death. We pray for everyone in the world.

On Good Friday we honor the cross. We may kiss it or touch it. We may genuflect or bow deeply in front of it. On Good Friday our celebration of Jesus' suffering, or Passion, and death ends with the Communion Service. We walk in procession to the altar and share in the Eucharist. We receive the Body of Christ.

At home we think about how Jesus suffered and died on this day. Our prayers help us to get ready for the joy of Jesus' new life at Easter.

# Prayers for the Whole World

*On Good Friday the Church prays a special Prayer of the Faithful. Pray this prayer of the faithful together.*

**Leader:** Let us pray for the Church.

**Child 1:** May God guide us and gather us in peace.

**All:** **Amen.**

**Leader:** Let us pray for the pope.

**Child 2:** May God help the pope to lead us as God's holy people.

**All:** **Amen.**

**Leader:** Let us pray for those who will soon be baptized.

**Child 3:** May God help them to follow Jesus.

**All:** **Amen.**

**Leader:** Let us pray for our government leaders.

**Child 4:** May God bless them and help them keep us safe and free.

**All:** **Amen.**

**Leader:** Let us pray for those in need.

**Child 5:** May God make their faith and hope in him strong.

**All:** **Amen.**

# Triduum/Easter

## Faith Focus

Why is Easter the most important season of the Church's year?

## The Word of the Lord

These are the Gospel readings for Easter Sunday. Ask your family to read the Gospel reading for this year with you. Talk about it with them.

Year A
  John 20:1–9 or
  Matthew 28:1–10 or
  Luke 24:13–35

Year B
  John 20:1–9 or
  Mark 16:1–7 or
  Luke 24:13–35

Year C
  John 20:1–9 or
  Luke 24:1–12 or
  Luke 24:13–35

## The Best Day of All

What is the best day of your life? Why do you say it is the best day you remember? For Christians Easter is the best day of all days. On this day God raised Jesus from death.

During Easter we remember that we are one with Jesus Christ, who is risen. For Christians every Sunday is a little Easter. Sunday is the Lord's Day. It is the day on which Jesus was raised from death to new life.

Easter and every Sunday are days of joy and celebration. On these days we remember that through Baptism we share in the new life of the Risen Jesus. We share in his new life now and forever.

# Celebrating Our New Life

**ACTIVITY** The earth is filled with signs that remind us of the gift of new life in Christ we receive in Baptism. Find and color the signs of new life in this drawing. With your family look for these and other signs of new life. Talk about what the signs you discover tell about Easter.

# The Second Week of Easter

## Faith Focus

Why are Christians called Easter people?

## The Word of the Lord

This is the Gospel reading for the Second Sunday of Easter. Ask your family to read it with you. Talk about the reading with them.

Year A, B, C
   John 20:19–31

## What You See

The Easter cross is a cross covered with a white cloth. The white cloth reminds us of the cloth that covered the body of Jesus. Draped over the cross, it reminds us that Jesus was raised from the dead.

## Easter People

Often we spend many days preparing for a big day. Then we celebrate it for one day and our celebration ends. The Church celebrates Easter much, much longer. We celebrate Easter for seven weeks.

During the weeks of Easter, we think about what it means to be baptized. We remember we have new life in Jesus. We think about what it means that Jesus is with us in the sacraments. We remember that Jesus is with us in all the baptized.

We are Easter people. We share the joy of Easter with God and with one another. We sing our song of joy, "Alleluia. Alleluia. Alleluia."

# Easter Joy

Share the joy of Easter with your family and friends. Use your favorite colors to make a beautiful Easter poster. Use these words that we pray aloud or sing at Mass, "Christ has died. Christ is risen. Christ will come again."

# The Third Week of Easter

What did the women followers of Jesus discover when they went to the place where he had been buried?

## The Word of the Lord

These are the Gospel readings for the Third Sunday of Easter. Ask your family to read the Gospel reading for this year with you. Talk about it with them.

Year A
Luke 24:13–35

Year B
Luke 24:35–48

Year C
John 21:1–19 or
John 21:1–14

## Sharing the Good News

Good news! What is your good news today? Christians have good news every day. Our good news is "Christ is risen!"

Early on the Sunday after Jesus died and was buried, Salome, Mary Magdalene, and the mother of James went to Jesus' tomb. To their surprise the stone in front of the opening of the tomb had been rolled away. A young man in a white robe said,

"You seek Jesus of Nazareth, the crucified. He has been raised; he is not here."      Mark 16:6

The women shared this good news about Jesus with Peter and other followers of Jesus. The women were the first to tell others that God had raised Jesus to new life. Their good news spread everywhere.

Today we proclaim the same good news about Jesus. We say, "Christ is risen. Alleluia!"

# Sharing the Good News!

ACTIVITY

*Think about what you have come to know about Jesus. Write or draw about that good news. Share your faith in the Risen Jesus with others.*

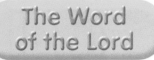

How did Saint Peter the Apostle share his faith in Jesus with others?

## The Word of the Lord

These are the First Readings for the Fourth Sunday of Easter. Ask your family to read the first reading for this year with you. Talk about the reading with them.

Year A
  Acts 2:14, 36–41

Year B
  Acts 4:8–12

Year C
  Acts 13:14, 43–52

## Saint Peter the Apostle

Sometimes we have something important to say. We want people to listen to us. We stand up and speak so everyone can hear us.

Fifty days after the Resurrection of Jesus, Peter the Apostle stood up in the marketplace in Jerusalem. After he got everyone's attention, Peter spoke out loud. He told everyone that Jesus, who died on the cross, was raised from the dead and was alive.

Peter traveled to many other places to tell people about Jesus. People listened to Peter. They believed what he said and were baptized. The number of people who believed in Jesus grew and grew.

# My Faith Community

ACTIVITY Your parish is your faith community. You learn about Jesus in your parish. Write the names of people in your parish who tell you about Jesus. Then write one thing you learned about Jesus from each person.

People                          What I learned

_____             _____

                               _____

_____             _____

                               _____

_____             _____

                               _____

*Choose one thing you learned about Jesus. Share it with someone. This week I will share this about Jesus with someone.*

_____

_____

# The Fifth Week of Easter

## Faith Focus

How did the early Church welcome its new members?

## The Word of the Lord

These are the Gospel readings for the Fifth Sunday of Easter. Ask your family to read the Gospel reading for this year with you. Talk about the reading with them.

Year A
  John 14:1–12

Year B
  John 15:1–8

Year C
  John 13:31–35

## Welcome!

When new children join your class, how do you help them feel welcome? Maybe you show them how to find the lunchroom. Or maybe you invite them to play with your friends.

The members of the early Church welcomed its new members in Baptism. They showed the new members they were welcome in many ways. They shared meals and prayed together. They rejoiced together and gave thanks.

Members of the early Church helped those who needed food, clothing, and shelter. By treating people this way, the Church treated people as Jesus did.

# Welcoming People
# as Jesus Would

*With a partner create a story about welcoming people as Jesus would welcome them. Write or draw your story in this space. Act out your story for the class.*

Welcome

Aloha! E Komo Mai

Bienvenida

Soo-dhawayn

# The Sixth Week of Easter

## Faith Focus

How did the early Christians tell others about Jesus?

## The Word of the Lord

These are the Gospel readings for the Sixth Sunday of Easter. Ask your family to read the Gospel reading for this year with you. Talk about the reading with them.

Year A
John 14:15–21

Year B
John 15:9–17

Year C
John 14:23–29

## Share the Good News

When the time came for the Risen Jesus to return to his Father, Jesus took his followers to a hillside. We call the return of the Risen Jesus to his Father the Ascension. Jesus told his disciples to tell others about him and to invite them to become his followers.

The Holy Spirit helped the followers of Jesus to share with others what Jesus said and did. Philip the Apostle went to Samaria to tell the people all about Jesus. Samaria was a place Jesus had visited.

When the other Apostles heard what Philip was doing, they sent Peter and John there too. Many people came to believe in Jesus and asked to be baptized.

# A Blessing Prayer

*Telling others about Jesus is the work of the whole Church. Pray this prayer and ask God to help you do that work.*

**Leader:** May the Lord bless your hands that you may help others.

**All:** **Amen.**

**Leader:** May the Lord bless your eyes that you may see the ways of God.

**All:** **Amen.**

**Leader:** May the Lord bless your lips that you may speak words of kindness.

**All:** **Amen.**

**Leader:** May the Lord bless your ears that you may hear God's word.

**All:** **Amen.**

**Leader:** May the Lord bless your feet that you may go forth to serve the Lord.

**All:** **Amen.**

**Leader:** May the Lord bless your heart that you may grow to be strong in love.

**All:** **Amen.**

# The Seventh Week of Easter

When does the Church gather to pray?

## The Word of the Lord

These are the Gospel readings for the Seventh Sunday of Easter. Ask your family to read the Gospel reading for this year with you. Talk about the reading with them.

Year A
John 17:1–11

Year B
John 17:11–19

Year C
John 17:20–26

## A Praying Church

This week we listen to a story that tells about Jesus praying for his followers. What Gospel stories do you know that tell about Jesus praying?

The followers of Jesus are people of prayer. Every Saturday evening and every Sunday the Church gathers all over the world to celebrate the Eucharist. The Church also gathers several times every day of the year to pray. We call this daily prayer of the Church the Liturgy of the Hours.

Morning prayer gets us ready to make our day holy. Evening prayer closes our day. We remember and thank God for all his blessings.

Throughout each day of the year all over the world the Church gathers to pray. We bless and thank God for what he has done for us. We ask God to care for his people, the Church, and for all people.

# My Daily Prayers

*Use the prayers on this page to make Morning Prayer and Evening Prayer prayer cards. Take the time to pray every morning and every evening.*

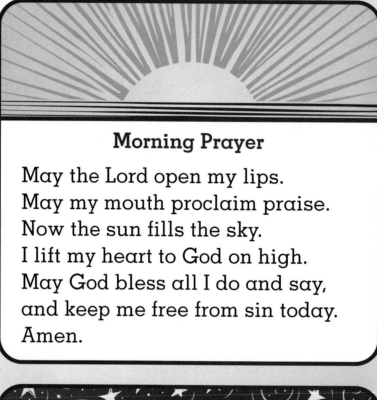

**Morning Prayer**

May the Lord open my lips.
May my mouth proclaim praise.
Now the sun fills the sky.
I lift my heart to God on high.
May God bless all I do and say,
and keep me free from sin today.
Amen.

**Evening Prayer**

Thank you, Lord, for this bright day.
Now, stay near. For this we pray.
Let your strong love surround us,
as darkness wraps all around us.
We leave to you, O God unsleeping,
this quiet world for your safekeeping.
Amen.

# Pentecost

## Faith Focus

Who helps us to live as followers of Jesus?

## The Word of the Lord

These are the Scripture readings for Pentecost. Ask your family to read one of the readings with you. Talk about the reading with them.

First Reading
 Acts 2:1–11

Second Reading
 1 Corinthians 12:3–7,
 12–13

Gospel
 John 20:19–23

## The Holy Spirit

What do you do when you have to do something that is very difficult to do? How do you feel when someone helps you?

Jesus knew that his disciples would need help to do the work he gave them to do. So he promised that the Holy Spirit would come and help them.

On the day of Pentecost, the Holy Spirit came to Peter the Apostle and the other disciples as Jesus promised. Peter was filled with courage. He told a crowd from many different countries that God had raised Jesus to new life. Everyone was amazed by what Peter was saying. Over 3,000 people became followers of Jesus that day.

The Holy Spirit is our helper and teacher too. The Holy Spirit helps us to tell others about Jesus and teaches us to live as followers of Jesus.

# Come, Holy Spirit

The Holy Spirit helps us to live as followers of Jesus. Unscramble the scrambled words in each sentence of this prayer. Write the missing letters of the words on the lines under each sentence. Pray the prayer to the Holy Spirit together.

**All:**      **Come, Holy Spirit, be our guest, in our work, be our (ster).**

<u>r</u> __ __ <u>t</u>

**Group 1:**      When we are hurt, **(lhea)** us.

<u>h</u> __ __ <u>l</u>

**Group 2:**      When we are weak, make us **(torsng)**.

__ __ __ <u>o</u> <u>n</u> <u>g</u>

**Group 1:**      When we fail, **(whas)** our sins away.

<u>w</u> __ <u>s</u> __

**Group 2:**      Bring us **(jyo)** that never ends.

__ __ <u>y</u>

**All:**      Amen.

# Catholic Prayers and Practices

## Sign of the Cross

In the name of the Father,
and of the Son,
and of the Holy Spirit. Amen.

## Glory Prayer

Glory to the Father,
    and to the Son,
    and to the Holy Spirit:
as it was in the beginning, is now,
    and will be for ever. Amen.

## Lord's Prayer

Our Father, who art in heaven,
hallowed be thy name;
thy kingdom come;
thy will be done on earth
    as it is in heaven.
Give us this day our daily bread;
and forgive us our trespasses
as we forgive those who trespass
    against us;
and lead us not into temptation,
but deliver us from evil.
Amen.

## Hail Mary

Hail Mary, full of grace,
the Lord is with you!
Blessed are you among women,
and blessed is the fruit
    of your womb, Jesus.
Holy Mary, Mother of God,
pray for us sinners,
now and at the hour of our death.
Amen.

## Act of Contrition

My God,
I am sorry for my sins
    with all my heart.
In choosing to do wrong
and failing to do good,
I have sinned against you
whom I should love above all things.
I firmly intend, with your help,
to do penance,
to sin no more,
and to avoid whatever leads me to sin.
Our Savior Jesus Christ
suffered and died for us.
In his name, my God, have mercy.

## Apostles' Creed

I believe in God,
  the Father almighty,
  creator of heaven and earth.

I believe in Jesus Christ,
  his only Son, our Lord.
  He was conceived by the power
    of the Holy Spirit
    and born of the Virgin Mary.
  He suffered under Pontius Pilate,
    was crucified, died, and was
    buried.
  He descended to the dead.
  On the third day he rose again.
  He ascended into heaven,
  and is seated at the right hand
    of the Father.
  He will come again to judge
    the living and the dead.

I believe in the Holy Spirit,
  the holy catholic Church,
  the communion of saints,
  the forgiveness of sins,
  the resurrection of the body,
  and the life everlasting. Amen.

## Nicene Creed

We believe in one God,
  the Father, the Almighty,
  maker of heaven and earth,
  of all that is, seen and unseen.

We believe in one Lord, Jesus Christ,
  the only Son of God,
  eternally begotten of the Father,
  God from God, Light from Light,
  true God from true God,
  begotten, not made, one in Being
    with the Father.

Through him all things were
    made.
  For us men and for our salvation
    he came down from heaven:
by the power of the Holy Spirit
  he was born of the Virgin Mary,
  and became man.

For our sake he was crucified under
    Pontius Pilate;
  he suffered, died, and was buried.
  On the third day he rose again
    in fulfillment of the Scriptures;
  he ascended into heaven
    and is seated at the right hand
    of the Father.
He will come again in glory to judge
    the living and the dead,
  and his kingdom will have no end.

We believe in the Holy Spirit, the
    Lord, the giver of life,
  who proceeds from the Father
    and the Son.
  With the Father and the Son he is
    worshiped and glorified.
  He has spoken through the
    Prophets.
  We believe in one holy catholic
    and apostolic Church.
  We acknowledge one baptism for
    the forgiveness of sins.
  We look for the resurrection of the
    dead, and the life of the world
    to come. Amen.

## Prayer to the Holy Spirit

Come, Holy Spirit, fill the hearts
   of your faithful.
And kindle in them the
   fire of your love.
Send forth your Spirit and
   they shall be created.
And you will renew the
   face of the earth.

## A Vocation Prayer

God, I know you will call me
for special work in my life.
Help me to follow Jesus each day
and be ready to answer your call.

## Morning Prayer

Dear God,
as I begin this day,
keep me in your love and care.
Help me to live as your child today.
Bless me, my family, and my friends
   in all we do.
Keep us all close to you. Amen.

## Evening Prayer

Dear God,
I thank you for today.
Keep me safe throughout the night.
Thank you for all the good I did today.
I am sorry for what I have chosen
   to do wrong.
Bless my family and friends. Amen.

## Grace Before Meals

Bless us, O Lord,
   and these your gifts
which we are about to receive
   from your goodness,
   through Christ our Lord.
Amen.

## Grace After Meals

We give you thanks for all your gifts,
   almighty God,
living and reigning now and for ever.
Amen.

# Rosary

Catholics pray the Rosary to honor Mary and remember the important events in the life of Jesus and Mary. There are twenty mysteries of the Rosary. Follow the steps from 1 to 5.

*3. Think of the first mystery. Pray an Our Father, 10 Hail Marys, and the Glory Prayer.*

*5. Pray the Hail, Holy Queen prayer. Make the Sign of the Cross.*

*2. Pray an Our Father, 3 Hail Marys, and the Glory Prayer.*

*4. Repeat step 3 for each of the next 4 mysteries.*

*1. Make the Sign of the Cross and pray the Apostles' Creed.*

## Joyful Mysteries

1. The Annunciation
2. The Visitation
3. The Nativity
4. The Presentation
5. The Finding of Jesus in the Temple

## Mysteries of Light

1. The Baptism of Jesus in the Jordan River
2. The Miracle at the Wedding at Cana
3. The Proclamation of the Kingdom of God
4. The Transfiguration of Jesus
5. The Institution of the Eucharist

## Sorrowful Mysteries

1. The Agony in the Garden
2. The Scourging at the Pillar
3. The Crowning with Thorns
4. The Carrying of the Cross
5. The Crucifixion

## Glorious Mysteries

1. The Resurrection
2. The Ascension
3. The Coming of the Holy Spirit
4. The Assumption of Mary
5. The Coronation of Mary

## Hail, Holy Queen

Hail, holy Queen, mother of mercy, hail, our life, our sweetness, and our hope.
To you we cry, the children of Eve; to you we send up our sighs, mourning and weeping in this land of exile.
Turn, then, most gracious advocate, your eyes of mercy toward us; lead us home at last and show us the blessed fruit of your womb, Jesus:
O clement, O loving, O sweet Virgin Mary.

## The Great Commandment

"You shall love the Lord, your God, with all your heart, with all your soul, and with all your mind. . . . You shall love your neighbor as yourself."

Matthew 22:37, 39

## Jesus' Commandment

"This is my commandment: love one another as I love you."

John 15:12

## The Ten Commandments

1. I am the LORD your God: you shall not have strange Gods before me.
2. You shall not take the name of the LORD your God in vain.
3. Remember to keep holy the LORD'S Day.
4. Honor your father and your mother.
5. You shall not kill.
6. You shall not commit adultery.
7. You shall not steal.
8. You shall not bear false witness against your neighbor.
9. You shall not covet your neighbor's wife.
10. You shall not covet your neighbor's goods.

Based on Exodus 20:2–3, 7–17

# The Seven Sacraments

Jesus gave the Church the seven sacraments. The seven sacraments are signs of God's love for us. When we celebrate the sacraments, Jesus is really present with us. We share in the life of the Holy Trinity.

### Anointing of the Sick

We receive God's healing strength when we are sick or dying, or weak because of old age.

### Baptism

We are joined to Christ. We become members of the Body of Christ, the Church.

### Confirmation

The Holy Spirit strengthens us to live as children of God.

### Holy Orders

A baptized man is ordained to serve the Church as a bishop, priest, or deacon.

### Eucharist

We receive the Body and Blood of Jesus.

### Matrimony

A baptized man and a baptized woman make a lifelong promise to love and respect each other as husband and wife. They promise to accept the gift of children from God.

### Reconciliation

We receive God's gift of forgiveness and peace.

# We Celebrate the Mass

## The Introductory Rites

We remember that we are the community
of the Church. We prepare to listen to the word of God
and to celebrate the Eucharist.

### The Entrance

We stand as the priest, deacon,
and other ministers enter the
assembly. We sing a gathering song.
The priest and deacon kiss the altar.
The priest then goes to the chair
where he presides over the
celebration.

### Greeting of the Altar and of the People Gathered

The priest leads us in praying the
Sign of the Cross. The priest greets
us, and we say,

**"And also with you."**

### The Act of Penitence

We admit our wrongdoings.
We bless God for his mercy.

### The Gloria

We praise God for all the good
he has done for us.

### The Collect

The priest leads us in praying the
Collect, or the opening prayer.
We respond, **"Amen."**

# The Liturgy of the Word
### God speaks to us today.
### We listen and respond to God's word.

**The First Reading from the Bible**
We sit and listen as the reader reads from the Old Testament or from the Acts of the Apostles. The reader concludes, "The word of the Lord." We respond,
**"Thanks be to God."**

**The Responsorial Psalm**
The song leader leads us in singing a psalm.

**The Second Reading from the Bible**
The reader reads from the New Testament, but not from the four Gospels. The reader concludes, "The word of the Lord." We respond,
**"Thanks be to God."**

**The Acclamation**
We stand to honor Christ present with us in the Gospel. The song leader leads us in singing **"Alleluia, Alleluia, Alleluia"** or another chant during Lent.

**The Gospel**
The deacon or priest proclaims, "A reading from the holy gospel according to (name of Gospel writer)." We respond,
**"Glory to you, O Lord."**
He proclaims the Gospel. At the end he says, "The gospel of the Lord." We respond,
**"Praise to you, Lord Jesus Christ."**

**The Homily**
We sit. The priest or deacon preaches the homily. He helps the whole community understand the word of God spoken to us in the readings.

**The Profession of Faith**
We stand and profess our faith. We pray the Nicene Creed together.

**The Prayer of the Faithful**
The priest leads us in praying for our Church and its leaders, for our country and its leaders, for ourselves and others, for the sick and those who have died. We can respond to each prayer in several ways. One way we respond is,
**"Lord, hear our prayer."**

# The Liturgy of the Eucharist

**We join with Jesus and the Holy Spirit
to give thanks and praise to God the Father.**

**The Preparation of the Gifts**
We sit as the altar table is prepared and the collection is taken up. We share our blessings with the community of the Church and especially with those in need. The song leader may lead us in singing a song. The gifts of bread and wine are brought to the altar.

The priest lifts up the bread and blesses God for all our gifts. He prays, "Blessed are you, Lord, God of all creation . . ." We respond,
**"Blessed be God for ever."**

The priest lifts up the cup of wine and prays, "Blessed are you, Lord, God of all creation . . ." We respond,
**"Blessed be God for ever."**

The priest invites us,
"Pray, my brothers and sisters, that our sacrifice may be acceptable to God, the almighty Father."

We stand and respond,
**"May the Lord accept the sacrifice at your hands for the praise and glory of his name, for our good, and the good of all his Church."**

**The Prayer over the Offerings**
The priest leads us in praying the Prayer over the Offerings. We respond, **"Amen."**

## Preface

The priest invites us to join in praying the Church's great prayer of praise and thanksgiving to God the Father.

Priest: "The Lord be with you."

**Assembly: "And also with you."**

Priest: "Lift up your hearts."

**Assembly: "We lift them up to the Lord."**

Priest: "Let us give thanks to the Lord our God."

**Assembly: "It is right to give him thanks and praise."**

After the priest sings or prays aloud the preface, we join in acclaiming,

**"Holy, holy, holy Lord, God of power and might.**
**Heaven and earth are full of your glory.**
**Hosanna in the highest.**
**Blessed is he who comes in the name of the Lord.**
**Hosanna in the highest."**

## The Eucharistic Prayer

The priest leads the assembly in praying the Eucharistic Prayer. We call upon the Holy Spirit to make our gifts of bread and wine holy and that they become the Body and Blood of Jesus. We recall what happened at the Last Supper. The bread and wine become the Body and Blood of the Lord. Jesus is truly and really present under the appearances of bread and wine.

The priest sings or says aloud, "Let us proclaim the mystery of faith." We respond using this or another acclamation used by the Church,

**"Christ has died, Christ is risen, Christ will come again."**

The priest then prays for the Church. He prays for the living and the dead.

## Doxology

The priest concludes the praying of the Eucharistic Prayer. He sings or says aloud,

**"Through him, with him, in him, in the unity of the Holy Spirit, all glory and honor is yours, almighty Father, for ever and ever."**

We respond by singing, **"Amen."**

I AM WITH YOU ALWAYS

# The Communion Rite

## The Lord's Prayer

The priest invites us to pray the Lord's Prayer together. He says,
"Let us pray with confidence to the Father in the words our Savior gave us."

Together with the priest we continue,
**"Our Father who art in heaven, hallowed be thy name; thy kingdom come; thy will be done on earth as it is in heaven. Give us this day our daily bread; and forgive us our trespasses as we forgive those who trespass against us; and lead us not into temptation, but deliver us from evil."**

The priest continues,
"Deliver us, Lord, . . . as we wait in joyful hope for the coming of our Savior Jesus Christ."

## Doxology

We end the prayer by praying the acclamation,
**"For the kingdom, the power, and the glory are yours, now and for ever."**

## The Rite of Peace

The priest invites us to share a sign of peace, saying, "The peace of the Lord be with you always." We respond,
**"And also with you."**
We share a sign of peace.

## The Fraction, or the Breaking of the Bread

The priest breaks the host, the consecrated bread. We sing or pray aloud,
**"Lamb of God, you take away the sins of the world: have mercy on us. Lamb of God, you take away the sins of the world: have mercy on us. Lamb of God, you take away the sins of the world: grant us peace."**

The priest, deacon, or extraordinary minister of Holy Communion holds up the host. We bow and the priest, deacon, or extraordinary minister of Holy Communion says, "The body of Christ." We respond, **"Amen."** We then receive the consecrated host in our hand or on our tongue.

If we are to receive the Blood of Christ, the priest, deacon, or extraordinary minister of Holy Communion holds up the cup containing the consecrated wine. We bow and the priest, deacon, or extraordinary minister of Holy Communion says, "The blood of Christ." We respond, **"Amen."** We take the cup in our hands and drink from it.

## The Prayer after Communion
We stand as the priest invites us to pray saying, "Let us pray." He prays the Prayer after Communion. We respond, **"Amen."**

## Communion
The priest raises the host and says aloud,

"This is the Lamb of God who takes away the sins of the world.
Happy are those who are called to his supper."

We join with him and say,

**"Lord, I am not worthy to receive you, but only say the word and I shall be healed."**

The priest receives Communion. Next, the deacon and the extraordinary ministers of Holy Communion and the members of the assembly receive Communion.

# The Concluding Rites

**We are sent forth to do good works,
praising and blessing the Lord.**

**Greeting**

We stand. The priest greets us as
we prepare to leave. He says, "The
Lord be with you." We respond,
**"And also with you."**

**Blessing**

The priest or deacon may invite us,
"Bow your heads and pray for
God's blessing."
The priest blesses us saying,
"May almighty God bless you,
the Father, and the Son,
and the Holy Spirit."
We respond, **"Amen."**

**Dismissal of the People**

The priest or deacon sends us
forth, using these or similar words,
"The Mass is ended, go in
peace."
We respond,
**"Thanks be to God."**

We sing a hymn. The priest and the
deacon kiss the altar. The priest,
deacon, and other ministers bow to
the altar and leave in procession.

# The Sacrament of Reconciliation

**Individual Rite**

Greeting
Scripture Reading
Confession of Sins
    and Acceptance of Penance
Act of Contrition
Absolution
Closing Prayer

**Communal Rite**

Greeting
Scripture Reading
Homily
Examination of Conscience, a
    litany of contrition, and the
    Lord's Prayer
Individual Confession
    and Absolution
Closing Prayer

# A Tour of a Church

Some churches are made of stone and some are wooden. Some are big and some are small. One thing they all have in common is that they are places where people worship God.

## Baptismal Font

The baptismal font is the pool of water used for Baptism. Water is used to remind us of new life. The tall candle is called the Easter candle. It is lit during Baptism to remind us of Jesus, the Light of the world.

## Assembly

The assembly is the people gathered for Mass. The pews are the seats where the people sit.

## Crucifix

The crucifix is a sign of Jesus' love for us. You see the crucifix near the altar. Not all crucifixes are the same. This one shows Jesus after he was raised from the dead. The crucifix reminds us that Jesus died and was raised again to new life.

## Altar

The altar is the table where the Liturgy of the Eucharist is celebrated at Mass. It reminds us of the Last Supper and that Jesus died for us. The altar is also called the Table of the Lord. It is the table from which Jesus shares his Body and Blood with us.

## Ambo

The ambo is the special stand or place from where the Scriptures are read during Mass. The lector is the person who reads the first and second readings during Mass. The deacon or priest reads the Gospel.

## The Book of the Gospels Lectionary

The Book of the Gospels contains the Gospel readings we listen to at Mass. The first two readings are read from the Lectionary.

## Tabernacle

The tabernacle is where the Eucharist, or Blessed Sacrament, is kept. When the candle next to the tabernacle is lit, it means that the Blessed Sacrament is in the tabernacle.

# Glossary

## A

absolution [page 124]
Absolution is the forgiveness of our sins in the sacrament of Reconciliation through the words and actions of the priest.

**almighty** [page 30]
God alone is almighty. This means that only God has the power to do everything.

almsgiving [page 177]
The word *almsgiving* means "sharing something to help the poor."

ambo [page 57]
The ambo is the place in the church where the word of God is proclaimed.

anoint [page 107]
Anoint means to bless a person with holy oil.

**Apostles** [page 70]
The Apostles were the disciples who Jesus chose and sent to preach the Gospel to the whole world in his name.

**Ascension** [page 78]
The Ascension is the return of the Risen Jesus to his Father in heaven forty days after the Resurrection.

assembly [page 131]
The assembly is the people who gather to celebrate the Mass.

## B

**Baptism** [page 106]
Baptism is the sacrament that joins us to Christ and makes us members of the Church. We receive the gift of the Holy Spirit and become adopted sons and daughters of God.

**believe** [page 14]
To believe in God means to know God and to give ourselves to him with all our heart.

> **The words in boldface type are Faith Words in the text.**

Bible [page 15]
The Bible is the written word of God. It is the story of God's love for us.

**Body of Christ** [page 86]
The Church is the Body of Christ. Jesus Christ is the Head of the Church and all the baptized are its members.

Body of Christ [page 148]
The consecrated bread at Mass is the Body of Christ. Through the words of the priest and the power of the Holy Spirit the bread and wine become the Body and Blood of Christ at Mass.

Book of Psalms [page 38]
The Book of Psalms is one of the forty-six books in the Old Testament.

## C

Catholics [page 86]
Catholics are followers of Jesus Christ who belong to the Catholic Church.

Church [page 86 and 87]
The Church is the Body of Christ and the new People of God.

**commandments** [page 174]
Commandments are rules that help us live holy lives.

**Communion of Saints** [page 86]
The Church is the Communion of Saints. It is the communion of all the faithful followers of Jesus on earth and those who have died.

confession [page 124]
Confession is telling our sins to the bishop or priest by ourselves in the sacrament of Reconciliation.

**Confirmation** [page 106]
Confirmation is the sacrament in which the gift of the Holy Spirit strengthens us to live our Baptism.

**conscience** [page 190]
Conscience is a gift from God that helps us to make wise choices.

**consequences** [page 190]
Consequences are the good or bad things that happen when we make choices.

contrition [page 124]
Contrition is being truly sorry for our sins.

**Covenant** [page 46]
The Covenant is God's promise always to love and be kind to his people.

creation [page 30]
Creation is everything that God has made.

**Creator** [page 30]
God alone is the Creator. God has made everyone and everything out of love and without any help.

crucifix [page 65]
A crucifix is a cross with an image of the body of Jesus on it.

**Crucifixion** [page 62]
The Crucifixion is the death of Jesus on a cross.

deacon [page 24]
A deacon is a baptized man blessed in the sacrament of Holy Orders to serve the Church and help bishops and priests.

disciples [page 138]
The people who followed Jesus were called his disciples.

**Eucharist** [page 146]
The Eucharist is the sacrament of the Body and Blood of Jesus Christ.

Eucharistic Prayer [page 147]
The Eucharistic Prayer is the Church's great prayer of thanksgiving that we pray at Mass.

evangelist [page 79]
The word *evangelist* means "one who announces the Gospel."

**faith** [page 14]
Faith is God's gift that makes us able to believe in him.

fruits of the Holy Spirit [page 161]
The fruits of the Holy Spirit are signs that show we are trying our best to live as children of God.

**Gospels** [page 70]
The Gospels are the first four books in the New Testament.

grace [page 158]
Grace is the gift of God sharing his life with us. It is also God helping us to make good choices to live as children of God.

**Great Commandment** [page 166]
The Great Commandment is to love God above all else and to love others as we love ourselves.

hallowed [page 226]
The word *hallowed* means "very holy."

heaven [page 64]
Heaven is living with God and with Mary and all the saints in happiness forever after we die.

holy [page 198]
Holy means sharing in God's life and love.

Holy Communion [page 147]
Holy Communion is receiving the Body and Blood of Christ in the Eucharist.

Holy Spirit [page 24]
The Holy Spirit is the third Person of the Holy Trinity.

**Holy Trinity** [page 22]
The Holy Trinity is one God in three Persons—God the Father, God the Son, and God the Holy Spirit.

**honor** [page 158]
To honor someone is to treat them with kindness, respect, and love.

hymns [page 42]
Hymns are songs we use to pray to God.

**Jesus Christ** [page 46]
Jesus Christ is the Son of God. He is the second Person of the Holy Trinity who became one of us. He is true God and true man.

**Jewish people** [page 166]

The Jewish people are the people God chose as his special people in the Old Testament. This is the name of the people to which Jesus belonged.

**kingdom of God** [page 226]

The kingdom of God is also called the kingdom of heaven.

**Last Supper** [page 138]

The Last Supper is the special meal that Jesus ate with his disciples on the night before he died.

**Liturgy of the Eucharist** [page 146]

The Liturgy of the Eucharist is the second main part of the Mass. The Church does what Jesus did at the Last Supper.

**Liturgy of the Word** [page 130]

The Liturgy of the Word is the first main part of the Mass. God speaks to us through the readings from the Bible.

**Lord's Prayer** [page 218]

The Lord's Prayer is another name for the Our Father.

**M-N**

**Mass** [page 130]

The Mass is the most important celebration of the Church. At Mass we worship God. We listen to God's word. We celebrate and share in the Eucharist.

**mercy** [page 48]

The word *mercy* means "great kindness."

**missionaries** [page 169]

Missionaries travel to teach others about Jesus Christ.

**mortal sin** [page 199]

Mortal sin is serious sin that causes us to lose the gift of sanctifying grace. We must confess mortal sins in the sacrament of Reconciliation.

**Nativity** [page 47]

The Nativity is the name of the Bible story about the birth of Jesus.

**O-P**

**original sin** [page 46]

The word *original* means "first." Original sin is the sin of the first humans by which they broke their promises to God.

**parable** [page 114]

A parable is a story that compares two things. Jesus told parables to help people know and love God better.

**parish** [page 17]

Our parish is our home in the Catholic Church.

**Passover** [page 138]

Passover is a holy time of the year for the Jewish people. Jesus celebrated the Last Supper with his disciples during Passover.

**penance** [page 124]

Penance is a prayer or good deed the priest asks us to say or do in the sacrament of Reconciliation. Doing our penance helps repair, or heal, the harm we have caused by our sins.

**Pentecost** [page 78]

Pentecost is the day the Holy Spirit came to the disciples of Jesus fifty days after the Resurrection.

**prayer** [page 210]

Prayer is raising our minds and hearts to God.

**prayer of praise** [page 38]

A prayer of praise gives honor to God for his great love and kindness.

**procession** [page 133]

A procession is people prayerfully walking together. Processions are prayers in action.

**prophet** [page 54]

A prophet in the Bible is a person who God chose to speak in his name.

**proverbs** [page 182]

Proverbs are short sayings that help us to make wise choices.

**psalms** [page 38]

Psalms are songs of prayer.

**Reconciliation** [page 122]
Reconciliation is a sacrament that brings God's gifts of mercy and forgiving love into our lives.

**Resurrection** [page 62]
The Resurrection is God's raising Jesus from the dead to new life.

sacrifice [page 149]
A sacrifice is a gift of great value we give out of love. At Mass we share in the sacrifice of Jesus.

sacramentals [page 101]
Sacramentals are objects and blessings the Church uses to help us worship God.

**sacraments** [page 98]
The sacraments are the seven signs of God's love for us that Jesus gave the Church. We share in God's love when we celebrate the sacraments.

**sanctifying grace** [page 198]
Sanctifying grace is the gift of God sharing his life with us.

sanctuary [page 133]
The word *sanctuary* means "holy place." The sanctuary is the place in the Church where we see the altar and the ambo.

Savior [pages 62 and 63]
A savior is a person who sets people free. Jesus freed us from sin by dying on the cross. Jesus is the Savior of the world.

**sin** [page 122]
Sin is freely choosing to do or say something that we know God does not want us to do or say.

Son of God [page 46]
Jesus Christ is the Son of God. He is the second Person of the Trinity who became one of us. Jesus is true God and true man.

**soul** [page 22]
Our soul is that part of us that lives forever.

**Temple in Jerusalem** [page 166]
A temple is a building built to honor God. The Jewish people in Jesus' time worshiped God in the Temple in Jerusalem.

temptation [page 228]
Temptation is everything that can lead us away from God's love and from living as children of God.

**Ten Commandments** [page 174]
The Ten Commandments are the laws that God gave to Moses that teach us to live as God's people.

trespass [page 228]
To trespass means to do or say something that hurts our friendship with God and with other people.

venial sin [page 199]
Venial sin is sin less serious than mortal sin that hurts our relationship with God and other people.

vocation [page 229]
The word *vocation* means "what we are called to do." God calls everyone who is baptized to live as a follower of Jesus.

**wise choice** [page 182]
A wise choice is a choice that helps us to live as children of God.

works of mercy [page 49]
The works of mercy are ways to be kind and loving to people as Jesus was.

**worship** [page 98]
Worship means to honor and love God above all else.

# Index

# Credits

Cover Design: Kristy Howard
Cover Illustration: Amy Freeman

**PHOTO CREDITS**
Abbreviated as follows: (bkgd) background;
(t) top; (b) bottom; (l) left; (r) right;
(c) center.

**Frontmatter:** Page 7, © Jerry Tobias/Corbis;
11 (tl), © Bill Frymire/Masterfile; 11 (cr),
© Artville; 11 (bl), © Bill Wittman.

**Chapter 1:** Page 13, © PictureQuest; 14 (l),
© Corbis; 14 (r), © PhotoDisc; 16 (t),
© Myrleen Ferguson Cate/Photoeditinc; 16
(b), © Richard Hutchins/Photoeditinc; 20,
© Digital Stock.

**Chapter 2:** Page 21, © The Crosiers/Gene
Plaisted, OSC; 22, © Bill Frymire/Masterfile;
25 (t), © Dennis Full/RCL; 25 (c), © Elaine
Thompson/AP/Wide World; 25 (b),
© Myrleen Ferguson Cate/ Photoeditinc; 28,
© PictureQuest.

**Chapter 3:** Page 29, © PictureQuest; 30
(all), © PhotoDisc; 36, © PictureQuest.

**Chapter 4:** Page 37, © Myrleen Ferguson
Cate/Photoeditinc; 44, © Punchstock.

**Chapter 5:** Page 45, 46, © The Crosiers/
Gene Plaisted, OSC; 49 (tr), © James L.
Shaffer; 49 (bl), Getty Images/Punchstock;
49 (br), © Steve Prezant/Corbis; 52,
© SuperStock.

**Chapter 6:** Page 53, © Myrleen Ferguson
Cate/Photoeditinc; 57 (all), © Eric
Williams/RCL; 60, © PhotoDisc.

**Chapter 7:** Page 61, © The Crosiers/Gene
Plaisted, OSC; 63, © Artville; 64, © Anthony
Jambor/RCL; 65, © Bill Wittman; 68, ©
Punchstock.

**Chapter 8:** Page 69, © The Crosiers/Gene
Plaisted, OSC; 73 (all), © Eric Williams/RCL;
76, © Brand X.

**Chapter 9:** Page 77, © Robert E. Daemmrich/
Stone; 80, © Cherie Mayman/RCL; 81 (all),
© Bill Wittman; 84, © PictureQuest.

**Chapter 10:** Page 85, © Bill Wittman; 86,
© Tony Freeman/Photoeditinc; 89 (all),
© The Crosiers/Gene Plaisted, OSC; 92,
© Myrleen Ferguson Cate/Photoeditinc; 95
(tl), © Eric Williams/RCL; 95 (tr), © David
Young-Wolff/Photoeditinc; 95 (bl), © Bill
Wittman.

**Chapter 11:** Page 97, © Myrleen Ferguson
Cate/Photoeditinc; 99 (tr), © Eric Williams/
RCL; 99 (bl), © Bill Wittman; 99 (br), ©
Tony Freeman/Photoeditinc; 101 (tr, bl), ©
The Crosiers/Gene Plaisted, OSC; 101 (br),
© Eric Williams/RCL; 104, © Michael
Newman/Photoeditinc.

**Chapter 12:** Page 105, © The Crosiers/Gene
Plaisted, OSC; 106, © Sam Martinez/RCL;
107 (all), © Dennis Full/RCL; 108, © Bill
Wittman; 112, © The Crosiers/Gene Plaisted,
OSC.

**Chapter 13:** Page 113, © Frank Siteman/
Stone; 120, © James Frank/PictureQuest.

**Chapter 14:** Page 121, © Bill Wittman; 122
(tr), © SuperStock Inc.; 122 (bl), © Jeff
Greenberg/Photoeditinc; 124, © Stephen
McBrady/Photoeditinc; 128, © PictureQuest.

**Chapter 15:** Page 129, © David Young-Wolff/
Photoeditinc; 130, © The Crosiers/Gene
Plaisted, OSC; 131, © Bill Wittman; 132,
133, © The Crosiers/Gene Plaisted, OSC;
136, © Bill Wittman.

**Chapter 16:** Page 137, © Anthony Jambor/
RCL; 141 (all), © Octavio A. Duran; 144,
© James L. Shaffer.

**Chapter 17:** Page 145, © The Crosiers/Gene
Plaisted, OSC; 146, © Donald F. Wristen/
RCL; 148, © Myrleen Ferguson Cate/
Photoeditinc; 149 (bl), © Comstock Klips;
149 (br), © Comstock Images; 152, © Eric
Williams/RCL; 155 (tl), © Milazzo/Maryknoll
Fathers & Brothers; 155 (cr), © Gettyimages/
Stone; 155 (bl), © Gettyimages/Punchstock.

**Chapter 18:** Page 157, © Robert Cushman-
Hayes; 158, © Shannon Stirnweis/SuperStock;
160 (t), © Getty Images/Punchstock; 160 (b),
© Ariel Skelley/Corbis; 161, © The Granger
Collection; 164, © Ariel Skelley/Masterfile.

**Chapter 19:** Page 165, © David Young-
Wolff/Photoeditinc; 169 (tl), © Fedora/
Maryknoll Fathers & Brothers; 169 (cr), ©
Milazzo/Maryknoll Fathers & Brothers; 172,
© Punchstock.

**Chapter 20:** Page 173, © The Crosiers/Gene
Plaisted, OSC; 174, © Paul Conklin/
Photoeditinc; 177, © Tony Freeman/
Photoeditinc; 180, © Comstock Klips.

**Chapter 21:** Page 181, © Lori Adamski
Peek/Gettyimages; 188, © Ron Chapple/
Gettyimages.

**Chapter 22:** Page 189, © Image Farm; 193
(l), © Bill Wittman; 193 (r), © Jeff
Greenberg/Unicorn Stock; 196, © Lisette
LeBon/SuperStock.

**Chapter 23:** Page 197, © RB Studio '96/The
Stock Market; 199, © Eric Williams/RCL;
201, © The Bridgeman Art Library
International, LTD; 204, © Digital Stock; 207
(tl), © Sisters of the Precious Blood; 207 (cr,
bl), © Myrleen Ferguson Cate/Photoeditinc.

**Chapter 24:** Page 209, © Angelo
Cavalli/Index Stock; 210, © Robert E.
Daemmrich/Stock, Boston; 212, © Ariel
Skelley/Corbis; 213, © The Crosiers/Gene
Plaisted, OSC; 216, © Myrleen Ferguson
Cate/Photoeditinc.

**Chapter 25:** Page 217, © The Crosiers/Gene
Plaisted, OSC; 218, © Garo Nalbandian/
Biblical Archeology Society; 221 (tr),
© MacDuff Everton/Corbis; 221 (cl), © Bob
Kriest/Corbis; 221 (br), © Sisters of the
Precious Blood; 224, © Bill Wittman.

**Chapter 26:** Page 225, © Tony Freeman/
Photoeditinc; 226, © Myrleen Ferguson
Cate/Photoeditinc; 227, © Kaz Chiba/
Gettyimages; 228, © Michelle D. Bridwell/
Photoeditinc; 232, © Myrleen Ferguson
Cate/Photoeditinc.

**Liturgical Seasons:** Page 235, (tl), © The
Grand Design Leeds, England/SuperStock;
235 (cr, bl), © Bill Wittman; 239, © Bill
Wittman; 241, © Kaz Mori/The Image Bank;
243, © Lori Adamski Peek/Stone; 244,
© PhotoDisc; 245, © Robert Harding Picture
Library/Biblical Archeology Society; 249,
© The Grand Design Leeds, England/
SuperStock, Inc; 251, © Christopher
Brown/Stock, Boston; 253, © Michael
Busselle/Stone; 255, © Donald F. Wristen/
RCL; 257, © Roseanne Olson/All Stock; 261,
© Bill Wittman; 263, © The Crosiers/Gene
Plaisted, OSC; 265, © PhotoDisc; 267,
© Gay Bumgarner/Stone; 269, © Ariel
Skelley/Corbis; 275, © Michael Newman/
Photoeditinc; 279, © Myrleen Ferguson
Cate/Photoeditinc; 283, © Myrleen Ferguson
Cate/Photoeditinc; 285, © Michael Newman/
Photoeditinc; 287, © Robert Cushman-
Hayes; 289, © Donald F. Wristen/RCL; 291,
292, © Bill Wittman; 293, © The Crosiers/
Gene Plaisted, OSC; 294, © Myrleen
Ferguson Cate/Photoeditinc; 295, © The
Crosiers/Gene Plaisted, OSC; 296, 297 (all),
© Anthony Jambor/RCL.

**ILLUSTRATION CREDITS**
Abbreviated as follows: (bkgd) background;
(t) top; (b) bottom; (l) left; (r) right;
(c) center.

**Frontmatter:** Page 8–9, Diana Craft; 12,
Yoshi Miyake.

**Chapter 1:** Page 15, Gary Torrisi; 17, Doris
Ettlinger; 19, Amy Freeman.

**Chapter 2:** Page 23, 26, Bob Niles.

**Chapter 3:** Page 33, Doris Ettlinger; 34,
Amy Freeman/Debi Friedlander; 35, Debi
Friedlander.

**Chapter 4:** Page 38, 39, Doris Ettlinger; 41,
Renee Quintal Dailey.

**Chapter 5:** Page 47, Doris Ettlinger; 48,
Gary Torrisi; 50, © 1966 The Order of Saint
Benedict.

**Chapter 6:** Page 54, 55, Yoshi Miyake; 56,
Jenny Williams; 59, Amy Freeman.

**Chapter 8:** Page 71, Gary Torrisi; 72, Yoshi
Miyake.

**Chapter 9:** Page 79, Margaret Lindmark.

**Chapter 10:** Page 87, Paula Lawson.

**Chapter 11:** Page 98, Gary Torrisi; 100,
© 1966 The Order of St. Benedict.

**Chapter 12:** Page 109, Pat Paris; 110, Debi
Friedlander.

**Chapter 13:** Page 115, Yoshi Miyake; 116,
Lane Gregory; 117, Mari Goering.

**Chapter 14:** Page 123, Bob Niles; 125,
Karen Maizel.

**Chapter 16:** Page 138, © 1966 The Order of
Saint Benedict; 139, Gary Torrisi; 140, Pat
Paris.

**Chapter 17:** Page 149, Jenny Williams; 150,
L.S. Pierce Illustration; 156, Gary Torrisi.

**Chapter 18:** Page 158, Shannon Stirnweis;
159, Gary Torrisi; 162, Debi Friedlander.

**Chapter 19:** Page 166, Mari Goering; 167,
Gary Torrisi; 168, Jenny Williams.

**Chapter 20:** Page 175, Doris Ettlinger; 176,
Jenny Williams.

**Chapter 21:** Page 185, Amy Freeman/ Debi
Friedlander.

**Chapter 22:** Page 194, L. S. Pierce
Illustration.

**Chapter 23:** Page 198, 203(b), Sally
Schaedler; 203(t), Debi Friedlander; 208,
Gary Torrisi.

**Chapter 24:** Page 214, Len Ebert.

**Chapter 25:** Page 219, Gary Torrisi; 220,
Pat Paris; 223, Karen Malzeke-MacDonald.

**Chapter 26:** Page 229, Doris Ettlinger.

**Liturgical Seasons:** Page 235, 237, Gary
Torrissi; 242, Dynamic Graphics, Inc; 246,
Doris Ettlinger; 247, Renee Quintal Dailey;
250, Chris Shechner; 258, Jo Arnold; 264,
Linda Yakel; 271, Margaret Lindmark; 272,
Linda Yakel; 273, Bob Niles; 277, Eulala
Conner; 280, Dynamic Graphics, Inc; 281,
Bob Niles; 286, Amy Freeman; 288, © 1966
The Order of St. Benedict.